FOUL DEEDS & SUSPICIOUS DEATHS
IN LEWISHAM & DEPTFORD

FOUL DEEDS AND SUSPICIOUS DEATHS Series

Wharncliffe's *Foul Deeds and Suspicious Deaths* series explores, in detail, crimes of passion, brutal murders and foul misdemeanours from early modern times to the present day. Victorian street crime, mysterious deaths and modern murders tell tales where passion, jealousy and social deprivation brought unexpected violence to those involved. From unexplained death and suicide to murder and manslaughter, the books provide a fascinating insight into the lives of both victims and perpetrators as well as society as a whole.

Other titles in the series include:

Foul Deeds and Suspicious Deaths in Bolton, Glynis Cooper
ISBN: 1-903425-63-8. £9.99

Foul Deeds and Suspicious Deaths in London's East End, Geoffrey Howse
ISBN: 1-903425-71-9. £10.99

Foul Deeds and Suspicious Deaths in & around Durham, Maureen Anderson
ISBN: 1-903425-46-8. £9.99

Foul Deeds and Suspicious Deaths in Hampstead, Holburn & St Pancras, Mark Aston
ISBN: 1-903425-94-8. £10.99

Foul Deeds and Suspicious Deaths in Colchester, Patrick Denney
ISBN: 1-903425-80-8. £10.99

Foul Deeds and Suspicious Deaths in Newport, Terry Underwood
ISBN: 1-903425-59-X. £9.99

Foul Deeds and Suspicious Deaths Around Derby, Kevin Turton
ISBN: 1-903425-76-X. £9.99

Foul Deeds and Suspicious Deaths in and Around Scunthorpe, Stephen Wade
ISBN: 1-903425-88-3. £9.99

More Foul Deeds and Suspicious Deaths in Wakefield, Kate Taylor
ISBN: 1-903425-48-4. £9.99

Foul Deeds and Suspicious Deaths in York, Keith Henson
ISBN: 1-903425-33-6. £9.99

Foul Deeds and Suspicious Deaths on the Yorkshire Coast, Alan Whitworth
ISBN: 1-903425-01-8. £9.99

Foul Deeds and Suspicious Deaths in Coventry, David McGrory
ISBN: 1-903425-57-3. £9.99

Foul Deeds and Suspicious Deaths in Manchester, Martin Baggoley
ISBN: 1-903425-65-4. £9.99

Foul Deeds and Suspicious Deaths in Newcastle, Maureen Anderson
ISBN: 1-903425-34-4. £9.99

Foul Deeds and Suspicious Deaths in Hull, David Goodman
ISBN: 1-903425-43-3. £9.99

Foul Deeds and Suspicious Deaths Around Newport, Terry Underwood
ISBN: 1-903425-59-X. £9.99

Please contact us via any of the methods below for more information or a catalogue.
WHARNCLIFFE BOOKS
47 Church Street – Barnsley – South Yorkshire S70 2AS
Tel: 01226 734555 – 734222; Fax: 01226 724438
E-mail: enquiries@pen-and-sword.co.uk
Website: www.wharncliffebooks.co.uk

Foul Deeds & Suspicious Deaths in
LEWISHAM & DEPTFORD

JONATHAN OATES

with historical introduction by
John Coulter

Series Editor
Brian Elliott

Wharncliffe Books

First Published in Great Britain in 2007 by
Wharncliffe Books
an imprint of
Pen and Sword Books Ltd
47 Church Street
Barnsley
South Yorkshire
S70 2AS

Copyright © Jonathan Oates 2007

ISBN: 978-184563-031-7

Typeset in 10/12pt Plantin by Concept, Huddersfield.

Printed and bound in England by Biddles.

Pen and Sword Books Ltd incorporates the Imprints of
Pen & Sword Aviation, Pen & Sword Maritime,
Pen & Sword Military, Wharncliffe Books,
Pen & Sword Select, Pen and Sword Military Classics
and Leo Cooper.

For a complete list of Pen & Sword titles please contact
PEN & SWORD BOOKS LIMITED
47 Church Street
Barnsley
South Yorkshire
S70 2BR
England
E-mail: enquiries@pen-and-sword.co.uk
Website: www.pen-and-sword.co.uk

Contents

Introduction

The aim of this book is to study in detail a number of serious crimes which occurred in Lewisham and Deptford from the late sixteenth century to the early twentieth. The time period has been chosen deliberately – and not because serious crime was particularly prevalent in these centuries (certainly not compared to the last half century). First it has been selected because, although an archbishop was murdered by Vikings sailing up the Ravensbourne at Deptford and assaults were being recorded on Blackheath in the fourteenth century, little is known about them. Secondly, although there have been many murders in Lewisham since 1938, I have thought these to be too recent as they are still in living memory for some. They are also too numerous. Finally, there is far more information available about earlier crimes because police files and other official data can be examined by researchers, unlike more recent and thus confidential information.

The book does not aim to be comprehensive, even within the limited time span which has been set. I have chosen cases which are varied and which are of interest. These include a discussion of a local man who has been suspected of being Jack the Ripper, the murder investigation in which a fingerprint was first used to convict killers, the death of a great Elizabethan playwright and a vicious murder of a young woman on Blackheath which has never been solved – until now.

Although some of the crimes chronicled here are not unknown, such as the killing of Marlowe in 1593 and the hitherto unsolved murder of Louisa Steele, the majority have not, to my knowledge, appeared in the many published histories of Lewisham and Deptford, of which there has been a renaissance of late. Nor have they been examined by writers of crime in London. Although previous writers of Lewisham and Deptford history have not neglected local crime, their attention has necessarily been drawn to many other key topics, such as transport, the growth of local communities and to social and economic life. Although serious crime is uncommon, it leaves bloody stains.

Researching for a book about crime is a little like detective work itself. The four major sources for this book are as follows. First, there are the files of the Metropolitan Police Force, held at the National Archives at Kew. These include witness statements taken by the police, confessions of criminals and correspondence of the police and police surgeons. None of this information has been published hitherto and, indeed, two of the files used have never before been open to public inspection (they were in part accessed by the author under the recent Freedom of Information legislation). Second, there is *The Times* digital archive, which provides an extremely useful way of searching two centuries of one of the country's leading newspapers. The newspaper reports for the nineteenth century and early twentieth century are very detailed. Third, there are the local newspapers, chiefly *The Kentish Mercury* (Lewisham was part of the county of Kent until 1889 and the newspaper retained the county title for decades) which are available at Lewisham Library. Because this is not indexed, a researcher needs the two former sources in order to find relevant cases and their dates. Once the latter have been ascertained, finding reports of crime is easy.

Finally, there are the miscellaneous sources. Speaking to the staff at Lewisham Local Studies Centre was of great use, as was a suggestion from the commissioning editor. Wide reading also helps – 'I am an omnivorous reader' remarked Sherlock Holmes and I have followed this dictum. Supporting works, such as the major works on Lewisham's history, gave useful background material. On the whole, most of the chapters in the books are the product of original research into primary sources, but the chapters concerning Marlowe and the Ripper are mostly the result of syntheses of recent works on these subjects. All these sources are listed at the end of the book.

One point is that I have not identified private houses which are associated with these crimes; they are only known by the street name. Should anyone wish to do so, ascertaining house numbers is relatively easy.

The author of this book was assistant archivist for the London Borough of Lewisham in 1994–1999 and so has some knowledge of the district's history. He has written another book in this series so is aware of the key sources for crime history. Although he has had no personal experience of serious crime, he did once reside in the same street in Catford as the murderer whose crime is chronicled in chapter 21, albeit seventy years later.

Those interested in fictional crime might be interested to know that there are a number of references in the Sherlock Holmes short stories to Lewisham. First, part of *The Man with the Twisted Lip* is set at The Cedars, Lee (which still exists), and much of *The Adventure of the Retired Colourman* is set at the fictional house, The Haven, Lewisham. There are references to 'that Lewisham gang of burglars' in *The Adventure of the Abbey Grange*. There are also allusions to Lee, Blackheath and Sydenham in other stories. Could this be because Conan Doyle's second wife, Jean, lived in Lee?

CHAPTER 1

Setting the Scene: Lewisham and Deptford to 1939

Deptford degenerated into a poor and crime-ridden suburb ...

ost of London's boroughs were the Frankenstein creations of the 1963 Local Government Act, which cobbled ill-assorted parts into ungainly wholes for the sake of administrative convenience or political advantage. Lewisham was formed in 1965 from the uneasy union of the industrialized and working-class town of Deptford with the still largely middle-class commuter suburb of Lewisham.

Until the sixteenth century Deptford had been an obscure fishing village on the Thames, better known as West Greenwich. Its more familiar name comes from the 'deep ford', long the lowest practical road crossing of the Ravensbourne, which was later spanned by Deptford Bridge. Until the eighteenth century the catering settlement by the bridge was quite distinct from the fishing and ship building community that grew up around the parish church of St Nicholas. It was the fact of it being a humble satellite of Greenwich that began the rise of Deptford from a village to a flourishing and wealthy town. King Henry VIII was greatly attached to his Greenwich birthplace, and had his favourite palace there. His ambition to be a major power in Europe depended on the creation of a strong navy. The first royal dockyard at Portsmouth was dangerously far from the London armouries, so in 1513 Henry founded the second and third at Deptford and Woolwich, where he could superintend them closely. Over the next century, as a pool of skilled workmen was established, the East India Company and various private individuals also set up shipyards at Deptford. Provisioning contractors for the Navy established depots, and anchorsmiths and ropemakers moved in. By the middle of the seventeenth century Deptford was a bustling and noisy naval town, full of inns, taverns and brothels.

The old parishes of Lewisham and Lee, which had been brought together by the London Government Act of 1899, were natural partners, as they shared a long boundary, and had a common history as farming communities turning slowly into dormitory suburbs. Lee was a narrow parish, stretching from Blackheath to Grove Park, but until the middle of the nineteenth century its small population was confined almost entirely to the northern quarter. To the south only a few farmers and farm labourers lived scattered among the woods and fields.

The parish of Lewisham was much larger than either Lee or Deptford, and a place of more importance in the Middle Ages. Its agricultural economy was varied by a little industry, based on the watermills of the Ravensbourne. In addition to the grinding of corn into flour, these were used for other activities useful to a farming community, such as the production of leather. In the eighteenth century cutlery, glassware and other goods for the London market were also manufactured at the various Lewisham mills.

The first commuters to settle in Lee and Lewisham were not businessmen working in London but courtiers attending on the kings and queens at Greenwich. They were succeeded in the second half of the seventeenth century by City merchants and bankers, who took over from the farmers as the leading citizens of the two parishes. As the eighteenth century matured, much of the farmland in the north of Lee and Lewisham was converted into the private parks of these incomers. By 1820 industry (except for corn milling) had entirely ceased, and the two parishes were inhabited by farmers, farm labourers, shopkeepers, retired people of means and wealthy commuters.

Deptford, 1770. London Borough of Lewisham

A View near the Red House, *Deptford in* KENT.   *Vue proche de la* Maison rouge, *à Deptford en* KENT.
Printed for Carington Bowles, Map & Printseller, N.º 69 in S.ª Pauls Church Yard, London. Published 1 Oct.ª 1770.

Deptford continued to grow and prosper throughout the eighteenth century, as the long succession of wars and the steady growth of British trade gave ample work to the shipyards. The old parish church of St Nicholas, near the Thames, was no longer adequate to the needs of the town even after it was enlarged in 1697, so Thomas Archer's splendid St Paul's, one of the Queen Anne churches, was built between 1717 and 1730. The division of Deptford into two parishes was carried out on the curious basis of equal rateable value rather than size, which meant that the new church received more than nine-tenths of the land (then mostly fields in New Cross and Brockley) and eventually grew to be ten times richer and more populous than St Nicholas. Those rural southern parts of St Paul's parish had more in common with Lewisham, on which they bordered, than with industrial Deptford, and they developed as commuter suburbs. New Cross was also a noted area for market gardens, which was another reason why its inhabitants looked to London rather than Deptford for their livelihood.

Deptford's great period ended in 1815, when the defeat of Napoleon inaugurated an age of peace and retrenchment. Orders for the public and private shipyards dried up, with serious consequences for the ancillary trades that depended on them. The artisans who had been earning good wages through all the long years of war were thrown out of work in large numbers. That in turn produced a

Deptford, 1771. London Borough of Lewisham

A View at Deptford, in KENT.   Vue à Deptford, in KENT.
Printed for Carington Bowles, Map & Printseller N°69 in St Pauls Church Yard, London. Published 1 May 1771.

crisis for the shops, and for the public houses that had been established on almost every corner during the prosperous days. Things got even worse in 1830, when the Royal Dockyard, after a decade confined to minor repair work, was mothballed. It was reopened in 1844, but soon proved unsuitable for the iron and armoured warships coming into use, and was closed finally in 1869. The private yards were also failing. In addition to economic difficulties, they were faced by the technical problem that the Thames was not wide enough for the safe launching of the larger ships now in request.

Salvation of a sort was at hand, for at this time of crisis Deptford chanced to become a major centre of communications. The banks of the Thames and Deptford Creek were becoming crowded with factories. Two canals had been cut through the town at the beginning of the nineteenth century and, although the Croydon Canal proved an instant failure, the Grand Surrey Canal attracted much commerce to its towpath. In 1836 the London and Greenwich Railway made Deptford the first suburb to enjoy a train service to the centre, and in 1839 the Croydon Canal was replaced by the London and Croydon Railway. Others lines quickly followed, and before long Deptford and New Cross were covered by a complex pattern of tracks, with industry filling the chinks that remained. But the jobs created were mainly unskilled, and the wages far less than the dockyard craftsmen had enjoyed. In particular, the canal and railway builders imported large numbers of Irish navvies, many of whom settled in Deptford, swelling the pool of cheap labour. The comfortable houses built for sea captains and shipwrights in the eighteenth century were broken up into slum tenements, and Deptford degenerated into a poor and crime-ridden suburb.

Improved Victorian transport was equally influential in the development of Lewisham and Lee, by making those suburbs possible places of residence for a wider and wider range of commuters. When private carriages or the expensive stage coaches were the only practical ways of getting to the City, very few could afford to live so far out. The first train services were not cheap enough for working men to use every day, but they did increase the attractions of Lewisham and Lee for the middle classes. The railway that came to Deptford in 1836 promoted development in the north of Lewisham. The London and Croydon Railway, opened in 1839, had stations at Sydenham and Forest Hill, leading to a building boom in the west. Trains came to central Lewisham and Blackheath in 1849, and to Lee in 1866, encouraging the creation of large houses anywhere within easy range of the stations. From the 1840s to the 1870s tall detached or semi-detached villas were the predominant building type in the district, but as train fares fell and bus services improved in the 1880s there was a

Lewisham Town Hall, c.1905. London Borough of Lewisham

Lewisham Clock Tower, c.1918. London Borough of Lewisham

change. Suddenly it was working-class terraces that were being built, often on the site of demolished eighteenth-century country houses. This new trend increased dramatically after 1890, when the first tram service in Lewisham began to run from Catford to Greenwich. From 1895 there were early morning workmen's trams, with a fare of 'one penny any distance'. The rich were now quitting Lewisham and Lee, leaving them to the middle classes and the respectable, regularly employed working classes.

The division of Deptford into the parishes of St Nicholas and St Paul in 1730 was perpetuated in 1900 when London was parcelled out into Metropolitan Boroughs. St Paul's parish became the Borough of Deptford but, to keep the populations more nearly equal, St Nicholas was added to the Borough of Greenwich as a make-weight. This unnatural separation of old and new Deptford still persists today in the London Boroughs of Lewisham and Greenwich, but the sensible local historian will ignore this artificial situation and treat Deptford as one and indivisible. The new Borough of Deptford was poor enough, even shorn of the riverside slums of St Nicholas, and became a favourite place for aristocratic charities, second only in popularity to the East End.

The First World War had little direct physical impact in Deptford or Lewisham, but its psychological and social effect was immense in reducing the availability of servants and increasing the pressure for

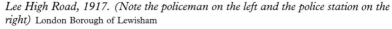

Lee High Road, 1917. (Note the policeman on the left and the police station on the right) London Borough of Lewisham

slum clearance and the provision of better homes for the poor. The shortage of servants accelerated the demolition of large houses, or their conversion into flats. There was little room for council housing estates in Deptford and the other inner South London boroughs, so all eyes were turned to the farmland that survived in the south of Lewisham. By persuasion and compulsion Lewisham's councillors and aristocratic landowners were induced to allow the London County Council to build its Bellingham and Downham cottage estates between 1920 and 1930. They added more than 40,000 working people to Lewisham's population, with far-reaching political consequences. In the 1930s Lewisham was a precariously genteel and conservative borough, requiring only some big event to change it forever. It did not have long to wait.

John Coulter

CHAPTER 2

Law and Order in Lewisham and Deptford

The first police were not popular and there was great hostility in some quarters towards them ...

Before a selection of crimes in Lewisham and Deptford is examined, it is necessary to have some knowledge of the forces of law and order which existed in the neighbourhood during the period in question, and the punishments available.

In Marlowe's time, and for centuries after, law and order was controlled by the parish, which, was, after all, the basic unit of 'local government', which also dealt with poor relief, the upkeep of the church and repair of roads and bridges. The parish vestry, made up of the more important men of the parish, would choose one or two men as constables, to serve for a year, unpaid, though expenses were allowed. These men did not need to possess any qualifications or experience whatsoever. This did not mean that they were all but useless, as has sometimes been implied. They were very variable in character – Joseph Cox in 1755 (featured in Chapter 4) was extremely astute.

Lewisham was part of the Hundred of Blackheath, an ancient jurisdiction which also covered Greenwich and Woolwich, among other parishes. The hundred had its own courts and constables and met four times a year. They mainly dealt with civil cases, such as the licensing of premises. However, by the nineteenth century, they began to fall into disuse. In any case, they could not try criminal offences, such as murder – these were for the County Quarter Sessions and the Assizes Courts.

One method of bringing criminals to book was the thief takers. These were men who captured criminals for reward money. They have an unsavoury reputation, as many were themselves thieves. Jonathan Wild, hanged in 1725, was a famous thief taker, as was his brother miscreant, McDaniel (detailed in Chapter 4). Yet the alternative – a professional police force of salaried officials – was seen as being far worse, as it would be both expensive and a potential system of corruption and tyranny.

Other methods were employed. Two Middlesex magistrates, Sir John Fielding and his half brother Henry, the novelist, were involved in the Bow Street Runners in the early 1750s. This was a small force of salaried men, both on foot and on horseback, who patrolled London and its environs. They had some successes in breaking up gangs and tracking down criminals. Yet some shared the defects of the thief takers, being hand in glove with the criminals, and in any case they were very few in number.

Watchmen were also employed, but were not always very effective. From 1699 to 1703, as many as thirty-two cases came before the magistrates of Deptford men 'not watching'. These watchmen would often be very elderly or poor labourers, already worn out by a day's labour, so it is not very surprising they were inefficient. Edward Richardson of Lewisham was so bad a watchman that in 1702 he found himself in the stocks, 'for neglect of office and not keeping watch'! Another watchman, Thomas Hawley (who appears in Chapter 8), was cowardly and drunken.

In the early nineteenth century, there were also other local efforts at preventing crime and detecting offenders. Parishes formed watch committees, who appointed watchmen and offered rewards for criminals. In 1837, the parishes of Lewisham, Lee, Kidbrooke and Charlton formed the United District Watch. A committee was formed to oversee patrols of former soldiers and discharged policemen (if of good character), who were em-ployed as constables and were

Lewisham Cage. London Borough of Lewisham

allocated regular 'beats'. It is un-certain how effective these men were, for although the committee had the approval of the regular police in R division, the minutes constantly refer to the men sleep-ing on their beats, being drunk or failing to turn up on time. In any event, it was disbanded in 1840 when the P division of the Metro-politan Police took over the re-sponsibility for law and order in the district.

The revolutionary step in crime prevention and detection was the formation of the Metropolitan Police in 1829 by Sir Robert

Peel, Tory Home Secretary. This was to create a salaried and professional quasi-military force of men, uniformed in blue and carrying
truncheons only (though cutlasses could be issued and inspectors
could carry pistols). They covered London, but in the district covered
by this book initially only Deptford was included, and it, along with
neighbouring parishes such as Greenwich, formed part of district R in
1830 (there were twenty-two districts in all). Ten years later, the force
was extended and Lewisham became part of P district. Unlike their
predecessors, their purpose was as much to deter crime as to detect it.

Blackheath Road Police Station was the headquarters of the police
in this district and opened in 1836, with a superintendent in charge.
The first known police station in the parish of Lewisham was Patrol
Place, Rushey Green, in 1846, then on Lewisham High Street, but by
the 1890s, it had moved to Ladywell Road, where it remained until
the beginning of the twenty-first century. There were smaller police
stations in Catford Hill, Howson Road, Brockley, Lee High Street
and Sydenham High Street (now Dartmouth Road).

The first police were not popular and there was great hostility in
some quarters towards them. In 1830, the toll keeper at Deptford
Creek Bridge charged two constables with violent assault as they
refused to pay the toll when they had to cross the bridge in pursuit of a
criminal. Six years later, one Gibbons was fined ten shillings for

Catford Police Station, c.1850. London Borough of Lewisham

assaulting a policeman in Deptford High Street. Worse was to come and two policemen were murdered in Deptford in the early nineteenth century (chronicled in Chapters 9 and 10). During the mass Chartist meetings on Blackheath in the 1840s, Chartists were deeply suspicious of the police presence. However, as the years passed, this antipathy among the law abiding towards the police force gradually subsided and the latter were seen as a useful and respectable method of detecting and preventing crime.

Yet they were not always successful in detection. Of the crimes chronicled here, there were four for which no one was convicted (though, as we shall see, often the killer(s) were known to the police) – and all occurred after the introduction of the Metropolitan Police. Some of the murders required no detective work – in a number of the cases to be outlined, the criminals simply gave themselves up.

Once a crime had been committed and/or suspects had been arrested, what then?

Suspects were often placed by the constable in the village lock-up or cage, a small structure designed to keep them secure until they were brought before the nearest magistrate. Depending on his decision, they might go free or they might be taken before a group of justices.

There was a Deptford Cage into which suspects in Chapter 6 were initially placed. Toll houses were often co-opted as lock-ups. In 1718, Andrew Miller, a Deptford toll keeper, was sworn in as a constable for the parish of Deptford, 'for the better apprehending and bringing persons to justice who shall in any way assault, abuse or affront him in the execution of his office'. The stocks and cage at Lewisham were on Watch House Green, off the High Street. The former was last used in 1835.

These cages fell into disuse in the nineteenth century – that of Deptford being no longer needed in 1855 as a police station was built in Deptford in Prince Street, moving to Amersham Vale in 1912. That of Lewisham had a rather more dramatic end. Two men were placed there. Both were drunk and one decided to have a smoke. Unfortunately this resulted in the straw catching fire, and before the constable could be found to unlock the cage the two were dead. Stocks could also be used to secure prisoners.

In the cases of manslaughter, suicide or murder, an inquest would have to be held. It might be adjourned for weeks, as in Chapter 23, if the police needed more time to find evidence, but usually it was held a few days after the death had occurred. A coroner and a jury of twelve local men (women could only become jurors in the twentieth century) would assemble in the locality. The body would be officially identified, usually by the next of kin. Medical evidence would be given by a surgeon, often a police doctor, to ascertain cause of death. Witnesses would give statements and clues were examined. If there was a suspect, he would be allowed to speak in his defence. The jury would then conclude with the type of offence and name the suspected guilty party if applicable.

Lewisham was part of the county of Kent. Minor criminals were brought before the Kent Quarter Sessions, who met four times a year. Criminals accused of serious crimes were brought before the Assizes, which met twice a year, once in spring and once in the autumn, at Maidstone, the county town. Lawyers would act for the Crown and for the defence, but the decision, though guided by the judge, was in the hands of the jury of twelve men.

However, and increasingly as the nineteenth century went by, Lewisham criminals appeared first at Greenwich Magistrates' Court. Evidence was given by witnesses and the jury would determine if the prisoner was to be charged, and if so, with what. If there was enough evidence, he would then be remanded for appearance from 1834 onward at the Central Criminal Court, known as the Old Bailey, in central London. They also found themselves incarcerated in Brixton Prison from the late nineteenth century as this gaol housed prisoners from all over what was now south London.

Punishments were variable. Generally speaking, prison sentences were rare until the late nineteenth century – prisons were seen as places to hold prisoners prior to trial. Capital punishment was used throughout the period chronicled by this book. Men could be hanged for other offences than murder and treason until the mid-nineteenth century. Theft of items valued over a shilling was a crime which could be punished by death. Yet although hanging was an option, transportation to the American colonies in the eighteenth century or Australia in the nineteenth became more common. This was either for life or for a fixed period of years. With the abolition of transportation in 1867, penal servitude, prison sentences with or without hard labour, was often given.

Yet even when criminals were found guilty of capital offences, death or transportation did not always result. They might be recommended for mercy by the jury, and if so, the judge passed on this request to the Home Secretary. Of 468 requests for mercy in England and Wales between 1900 and 1949, 348 were decided in the prisoners' favour. Men could be given gaol sentences, as in Chapter 24. If they were found to be insane, as several of the killers chronicled here were, they were sent to Broadmoor Asylum, which was built in Berkshire and opened in 1863. Following the introduction of the McNaghten Rules in 1843 (named after Daniel McNaghten, a lunatic who tried to kill Peel in 1843 and ended up slaying the premier's secretary instead), any man found guilty of murder, but who was unable to distinguish right from wrong, was classified as a criminal lunatic and detained at Her (or His) Majesty's Pleasure. This almost always meant that they were sent to Broadmoor until they died or recovered.

Such then were the forces of law and order in Lewisham in the past, and the methods of catching and punishing criminals. They were certainly not infallible. Their successes were often variable. But they were a bulwark that the law-abiding populace depended upon.

CHAPTER 3

The Mysterious Death of Christopher Marlowe 1593

... a mortal wound above his right eye to the depth of two inches ...

The death of the young Elizabethan playwright, Christopher Marlowe, is shrouded in mystery. It will probably never be entirely cleared up, as with the case of Jack the Ripper (discussed in Chapter 13). But some of the misconceptions can, at least, be dealt with. Marlowe and his death are certainly well known in fiction and fact. The novel *A Family Arsenal* (1976) by Paul Theroux contains the following snatch of dialogue:

> *'Deptford! ... Deptford!'*
> *'It's not too bad', said Brodie ...*
> *'Deptford! Marlowe was stabbed there – in a pub!'*
> *Murf said, 'Well, it's a rough area'.*

It certainly was. Moreover, in the film, *Shakespeare in Love* (1998), set in 1593, Marlowe is one of the characters (played by Rupert Everett), but only appears in two scenes. In the second, Marlowe rushes away from a meeting in London with a fellow playwright to his doom. His death is referred to, though not shown, and it is said he was killed in an argument over a bill in a tavern brawl in Deptford. It is noted that Marlowe attacked a man and then was killed by his own dagger being turned upon him.

So much for fiction. It is now time to examine what we know of his death.

On Wednesday 30 May 1593, four men, Robert Poley, Ingram Frizier, Nicholas Skeres and Marlowe, met at Mrs Eleanor Bull's house on Deptford Strand, which adjoins the south side of the Thames, near St Nicholas' Church. Recent scholars have been at pains to point out that Mrs Bull's house was not a pub as previous writers have claimed. They observe that it was not described as such in the inquest, and point to Mrs Bull's social standing and suggest it

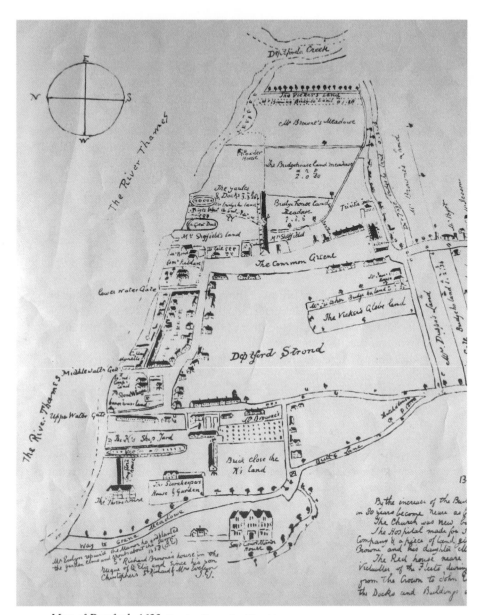

Map of Deptford, 1623. London Borough of Lewisham

was a victualling or boarding house, but the difference between these and inns/pubs seems merely a matter of words. The reference in the inquest to 'le recknynge' surely refers to payment being necessary for the food and drink consumed and thus to an inn or alehouse. It seems probable that the men hired out a room in an inn for their meeting, and paid for food and drink. As we know so very little about alehouses in Deptford as this time, this is a point that can never be entirely clarified.

One account suggests that Frizier invited Marlowe along. Mrs Bull was a widow of a respectable Herefordshire family, with connections at court. By the end of that day, one of the four was dead. It is worth spending some time in examining who these four men were.

Poley had, like Marlowe, been at Cambridge. He had been working as a spy for many years, having been involved in entrapping the Babbington plotters in the previous decade, though he had not always been trusted by Sir Francis Walshingham, Secretary of State and creator of an extensive intelligence network. He had worked in France in the 1580s, but now was operating in Scotland. Currently he was employed by Sir Robert Cecil, a rising star in the government and at court.

Frizier was the business agent of Thomas Walshingham, the latter being a cousin of the statesman just referred to. Frizier was also involved in shady deals of his own, though not ones which were always successful. Skeres was Frizier's henchman. He may have been involved in low-level espionage during the 1580s and he too had been involved in the Babbington affair.

And finally there was Marlowe. Born in Canterbury in 1564, the same year as Shakespeare, his parents were John, a shoemaker, and Katherine, his wife. He attended the King's School in Canterbury, and then Corpus Christi College, Cambridge. Whilst he was an undergraduate, two main developments occurred, both of which were to have immense importance for his future career.

First he began to make his mark in literature. He wrote his first play, *Dido, Queene of Carthage*, at about this time, as well as translating Ovid's *Amores*. He also entered into the pay of the government. In a report, his undisclosed work was praised thus,

> *in all his accions he had behaved himself orderlie and discreetlie, whereby he had done her Majestie good service & deserved to be rewarded for his faithfull dealinge.*

We do not know exactly what services Marlowe performed. It seems he did a good job, though. He may have been abroad, perhaps in the Low Countries or France, taking messages to and from other agents. Or he may have been spying on Catholics at Cambridge and elsewhere. Espionage was not a full-time activity for Marlowe or most spies at this time. They tended to be part-time, casual agents, who would be employed when required.

The later years of the sixteenth century were ones of political peril for England. Spain was at war with her – the Armada of 1588 being but one of the invasion attempts made. English aid was being sent to the insurgents in the Low Countries against the Spanish. At home, many Catholics were sympathetic towards the Spanish cause. Quite apart from this, there was religious controversy, with Catholics and Puritans at daggers drawn. Furthermore, there was the heated question of who should succeed the Virgin Queen.

Marlowe graduated with a BA in 1584, though not a particularly good one, and obtained an MA three years later. In the next few years, he achieved fame as a playwright. His great works include *Tamburlane the Great*, *Dr Faustus*, a cynical Machiavellian drama, *The Jew of Malta*, and *Edward II*, with its homosexual overtones. Richard Baines, an informer, later claimed, amongst other matters, that the dramatist said, 'all they that love not tobacco or boies are fooles'. These works were successful, but were also controversial because of the cynical attitudes shown concerning religion.

In 1591, Marlowe's services were again required on the behalf of the state. He went to Flushing in Holland and was eventually arrested there on the charge of coining and deported to England in about January 1592. Baines had betrayed Marlowe and claimed that he was planning to defect to the Spanish. Fortunately for him, these charges of treason were dropped and by May 1592 Marlowe was free again. What he was actually doing in Flushing is unclear, but the fact that he was freed after such serious accusations were made against him suggests that he was undertaking a task for the government.

The next, and last, twelve months of Marlowe's life, were full of accusations. He was said to be a heretic – a grave offence in any Christian country at that time – and, of lesser importance, alleged to be homosexual. He was also accused of penning anti-immigrant propaganda (Protestant refugees from Europe now resident in England were not popular with some). Whatever the truth of all of these, Marlowe certainly attracted the interest of the state. So much so that, on 18 May 1593, the Privy Council ordered him to make regular attendance on them. We do not know quite why this was. But, although Marlowe may have lived under a shadow at this time, he had a degree of freedom, residing at Scadbury Manor, home of his patron, Thomas Walsingham, which was near Orpington.

As said earlier, the four men met at Mrs Bull's in Deptford. All had links with the murky world of espionage and the Elizabethan under-world. Marlowe himself was no stranger to violence, having been previously involved in at least two brawls. For what happened next, we have only the report of the coroner's hearing, which is dependent on the three others. It is uncertain how truthful the account was, but as it is the only one, it must be examined.

They met at ten o'clock in the morning. At first all seemed to be peaceful, as the inquest notes:

there passed the time together and ate lunch, and after lunch were in quiet sort together & walked in the garden of the said house until the sixth hour after noon of the same day, and then returned from the said garden to the room mentioned, and there and in company dined.

We do not know what they talked about and can only speculate as to why the meeting took place. It is possible that Poley wished to talk to Marlowe about the playwright going to Scotland as a spy. Certainly the situation in Scotland was critical, with a possible Spanish invasion, abetted by dissident Scottish noblemen. Frizier may have suggested meeting at Deptford to save Walshingham having to entertain agents. As noted, it may have been he who invited Marlowe.

Yet in the evening it appears that relations openly soured. As the coroner noted:

it befell that after dinner the aforesaid Ingram and the said Christopher Morley [Marlowe's name was variously spelt] *were in speech & offered one to another divers malicious words, because they could not concur nor agree on the payment of the sum of pence, which is to say, le recknynge.*

It is possible that Frizier provoked the quarrel because he was concerned that Marlowe's association with Walshingham was damaging the latter, and Frizier's chances of financial gain depended on Walshingham. If Marlowe were removed from the scene – and it should be recalled that the rumours and accusations about him in the recent year were making him appear to be a disreputable character – then Frizier might benefit as his patron's star soared. He certainly seems to have had a motive.

According to the coroner, the quarrel, if quarrel there were, became physical.

And the said Christopher then lying on a bed in the room where they dined, and moved by an anger towards the foresaid Ingram Frysar because of the aforesaid words that had passed between them, and the aforesaid Ingram ... could in no way flee, it happened that the aforesaid Christopher Morley suddenly and with malice aforethought towards the aforesaid Ingram, then and there maliciously unsheathed his dagger of the aforesaid Ingram, which was visible at his back, and with the same dagger then and there maliciously gave the aforesaid Ingram two wounds on his head of the length of two inches and in depth a quarter of an inch.

Frizier claimed that he could not run because he was sitting on a bench between Skeres and Poley and so he had no alternative but to fight back.

> *And so it occurred in that affray that the said Ingram, in defence of his life, and with the aforesaid dagger of the value of twelve pence, gave the aforesaid Christopher then and there a mortal wound above his right eye to the depth of two inches in depth and in breadth one inch, of which the same mortal wound the said Christopher then and there instantly died.*

Marlowe was dead and Frizier had killed him. There is no doubt about that. But it is unlikely that Marlowe died instantly as the witnesses stated. He probably lived for a few minutes, and one source suggests he cursed to the last. After the killing, Frizier made no attempt to flee. Perhaps he knew that he would not be in danger of the capital sentence.

The inquest was held on 1 June. William Danby, the royal coroner, presided. This was because he automatically oversaw all inquests which fell within twelve miles of the Queen's person. Although the county coroner did not attend, this is not necessarily sinister, for he often did not attend inquests which were in Danby's jurisdiction. The jury, which was mainly made up of men residing in Deptford and Lewisham, together with Danby, examined the scene of the crime and the dagger. They agreed with Frizier's version of events and that he slew Marlowe only in self-defence. He was acquitted of murder and was a free man. Later in the month he received a royal pardon.

The account of the murder as supplied at the inquest does raise questions. If Marlowe attacked Frizier, why did Poley and Skeres not restrain him and so stop the fight? Why did they lie about the playwright being killed instantly? Perhaps they were taken by surprise and in a state of temporary shock (the fight was probably over very quickly). Or perhaps they were not averse to Marlowe's death. They may then have concocted a story between them which satisfied the coroner. But we do not know why. As noted, Frizier had a motive to kill Marlowe, but Poley may have wanted him as a live spy. The relationship between the three is unclear and will probably never be known for certain.

Marlowe was buried on the day of the inquest at the parish church of Deptford, St Nicholas, in an unmarked grave. Unfortunately, the entry in the parish register read that Marlowe had been 'slaine by Ffrancis Ffrizer'! To compound this, a later vicar referred to Marlowe's murderer as Francis Archer! Still other early accounts of his death were also inaccurate – one stating he was killed in a brawl on a London street and another that a serving man killed him.

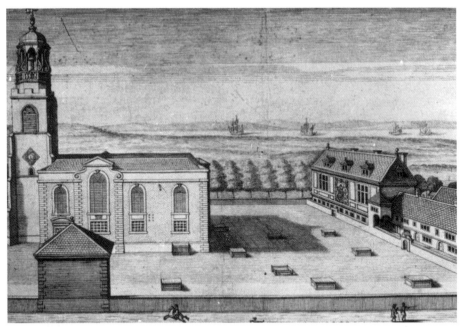

St Nicholas's, Deptford, c.1700. Burial place of Christopher Marlowe in 1593.
London Borough of Lewisham

As with the assassination of John Kennedy in 1963, conspiracy theories have abounded as to what really happened, and why. Marlowe was a controversial figure and he was involved in espionage. But it seems that major figures in the state, such as Lord Burghley, Cecil, the earl of Essex and Sir Walter Raleigh, did not benefit by his death. It may have inconvenienced Cecil as he may have been planning to have Marlowe undertake spying work in Scotland. A wilder theory is that Marlowe was not killed, but was spirited away and wrote the plays usually attributed to Shakespeare.

Others have suggested that Marlowe was killed because he allegedly knew of Sir Walter Raleigh's atheism, but all London in the know was already aware of this. It has been suggested that Audrey Walshingham, Thomas's wife, who had links with Frizier, might have had Marlowe killed in order to advance the Walshingham interest, but she did not marry him until years later. Another possibility is that Marlowe was a pawn in the larger power struggle between Essex and Cecil, and Skeres, who was one of Essex's men, may have been deputed to kill him.

Another possibility was that Marlowe was killed as part of a wider campaign against atheists, which commenced on 26 March 1593 with the creation of a new Royal Commission to act against them. Atheists were thought to be dangerous because they were apathetic towards the Queen's government, which was sanctified by the Protestant Church. Various informers and others said that Marlowe had penned atheistic tracts and some of his anti-heroes in his plays had made such remarks. On 11 May, Thomas Kyd, a friend of Marlowe, may have implicated him thus. It has to be said, though, that to murder him in such a convoluted fashion seems unnecessarily complex a method.

Or it could have been simply a case of men falling out over a bill. It is, after all, not uncommon for young men to fight in pubs, especially when fuelled by alcohol, if a contentious subject arises, and for the result to be deadly.

The truth is that we will never know what really happened and why the four men acted as they did. It seems probable that the inquest's findings were far from complete. But as to why one can only speculate.

The three others in Marlowe's company on that fatal evening had varying fortunes. Frizier seems to have prospered. By the time of his death in Eltham in 1617, he had become a respected member of the community, being a churchwarden and tax collector. Skeres did less well. He perhaps returned to the earl of Essex's service, but was gaoled after his master's failed *coup d'état* of 1601 and no more is heard of him. Poley remained in the espionage business until at least 1601; we do not know what happened to him.

Although it is probably of no consequence to Marlowe, his fame has outlived him for centuries, though it was only in the nineteenth that his work began to be regularly performed. He continues to fascinate us, by both his plays and his enigmatic life and death. Few have heard of Poley, Frizier, and Skeres, except in connection with Marlowe's death.

As for the film *Shakespeare in Love*, the references to Marlowe's death unquestioningly assume that the inquest's findings were accurate. As ever, the veracity of fiction should always be questioned.

CHAPTER 4

The Deptford Conspiracy 1755

... McDaniel once got a long knife and threatened to cut my throat ...

The story related here not only concerns crime, but is a commentary, or rather, a critique, of the system of detection and criminal justice prevalent in the eighteenth century.

It apparently all began on 29 July 1755. Three petty criminals from London set out to rob a fourth man near Deptford. The miscreants were Thomas Blee, a servant whose brother John had been transported for pick-pocketing in 1751, Peter Kelly and John Ellis. Kelly was nineteen, Ellis was a twenty-year-old chimney sweep, 'but they were both idle fellows, and had been used to pick pockets'.

The three rogues met at an alehouse in Little Britain, near St Paul's Cathedral. Blee bought bread and cheese for his compatriots, then they all went to the borough, on their way to Deptford calling at the Bell in Southwark. They drank a little gin here. Kelly pointed out one John Berry to Blee, observing, 'There is that thief-catching son of a bitch, your old master.' Blee replied, 'Never mind that, I do not belong to him now.'

There was more eating and drinking on their way to Deptford. In the early evening, the trio were at the Sign of the Ship in Deptford. Their intended victim, James Salmon, a leather-breeches-maker of Drury Lane, was also there. Salmon appeared to be the worst for wear for drink and talked about travelling back to London. At dusk he set out on his journey. Blee and his accomplices followed him and caught up with Salmon at the Four Mile Stone. Blee noticed that Salmon stopped at that point. He said to Kelly and Ellis, 'There is the old breeches maker. He is drunk, let us rob him.'

Kelly approached Salmon and asked him what he had under his arm. Even before any threat of violence had been made, Salmon seemed so frightened that he offered no resistance and replied, 'Gentlemen, take what I have, but do not use me ill.' Blee was immediately given the bundle. This contained two pairs of breeches.

Dover Castle, Deptford, c.1800. London Borough of Lewisham

Blee gave these to Kelly, but it was not enough and he asked Salmon, 'What money have you got?' The obliging Salmon told them, 'What money I have is in a tobacco box in my waistcoat pocket'.

Kelly put his hand in his victim's pocket and found the tobacco box, together with a clasp knife and fork. The three then ran as fast as they could back to London. They reached a lodging house at eleven o'clock in Kent Street, in which Blee had already paid for rooms. On the following morning, they came to the Spread Eagle pub, which they had visited on the previous day en route to Deptford.

Blee went to a nearby inn, the White Bear. He was not gone for long, and returned to the Spread Eagle for breakfast on lambs' livers with Ellis and Kelly. At this point, one James Egan, a shoemaker of Drury Lane, entered. Blee, who knew this man, said of him, 'That man deals in Rag Fair, a thousand to one but he'll buy the breeches, let us ask him.'

Blee addressed him, 'Master, will you buy some leather breeches?' Egan wanted to see them. He then agreed to pay five shillings for both, and gave a shilling deposit, claiming he would return in an hour with the rest of the money. A shilling was a labourer's daily wage at this time. But before he left, he shared, at Blee's insistence, their breakfast of liver and bacon, and then decided to enjoy a pipe of tobacco. But when he looked in his pockets, he exclaimed, 'Bless me, I do not know what I shall do – I have lost my tobacco box.'

Blee then whispered to Kelly, 'Let us sell him the box?' At first Kelly refused, for it was a striking box, but eventually he produced it and it was sold for a quart of two penny liquor, and Egan soon departed.

Blee left the room too, telling the other two he needed to have a shave. He soon returned, unshaven, remarking that the barber was busy. Eventually he left them and did not return, travelling as fast as he could towards the distant town of Uxbridge. Kelly and Ellis then had to wait for Egan and the rest of the money he promised them for the leather breeches. He arrived at last, but before he could pay them Stephen McDaniel, a London thief taker and a Holborn publican, arrived on the scene. It will be recalled from Chapter 2 that thief takers were men who made a living from arresting criminals for reward money.

He approached Kelly and said, 'Come out you blackguard, come out.' He seized Kelly by the collar, but James Cornack, a drummer, who was also in the pub, decided to intervene. He was offended by McDaniel's apparently unprovoked assault and asked sternly what it was about. However, when McDaniel told him he had a warrant for Kelly's arrest, the drummer told him, 'I'll not assist him, but you.' McDaniel tied the two up with rope and then questioned Egan. Egan was surly and replied, 'What is that to you, whatever it is, it is mine, for I have just bought it.'

McDaniel would not take no for an answer, and examined the bundle. In it he found the ill-gotten gains of the previous day's robbery. When Salmon arrived, he recognized the property as his because there were special identifying marks on the breeches and on a handkerchief.

McDaniel, presumably with the assistance of another, then took his captives to Greenwich in order to hand them over to a justice of the peace and, just as importantly, claim his reward. This would amount to £20 as the reward offered by the inhabitants of East Greenwich, as well as other rewards payable for the arrest of any criminals in or near the capital. He told Kelly and Ellis that if they confessed their crime to him he would untie them, they could travel to Greenwich by river and he would do all in his power for them. The two refused, so they had an unpleasant and slow journey to Greenwich instead. After a justice had been located, he agreed to commit the two to the county gaol in Maidstone, in order to await trial for highway robbery – which could result in the death penalty. A constable escorted them to Maidstone.

The trial took place at Maidstone at the Assizes for the Home Counties on 8 August. Those also present included McDaniel,

Deptford from the Thames, eighteenth century. London Borough of Lewisham

Salmon and Egan who would be principal witnesses for the prosecution. Salmon told the court that he had been robbed of the breeches and other possessions. Egan said that he was a dealer in old clothes and had been on the look out on the day after the robbery for goods to buy. He happened to be in Kent Street, visiting the Lock Hospital, and went into the Spread Eagle for refreshment. However, he met Blee, Kelly and Ellis, and examining their goods recognized them as Salmon's, as he had hitherto worked for him for many years. Therefore, whilst pretending to leave to obtain sufficient money to buy them, he went in search of McDaniel, who he knew would be able to have them arrested. McDaniel had nothing to add, but merely confirmed all that Egan had said.

Kelly and Ellis were found guilty on the evidence offered to the court. They would be hanged in due course of law. Meanwhile McDaniel was pleased with the rewards about to be his for his successful apprehension of two criminals. A success for the eighteenth-century system of thief taking, it would seem, despite McDaniel's sordid motives.

But then there came a crucial and startling new development. Enter one Joseph Cox, chief constable of the lower division of Blackheath. He had attended the trial at Maidstone and, just as the verdict was given, caused McDaniel, Salmon, Egan and Berry to be arrested, by virtue of the warrants he had carried down with him for that purpose. Cox had uncovered a conspiracy which will now be revealed.

After McDaniel had taken his two prisoners down to Greenwich, they were escorted to Maidstone by a Greenwich constable. Cox had spoken to this man and learnt from him that one Blee was also involved in the theft. Cox knew that McDaniel and Blee were acquainted and began to become suspicious of the whole affair. He made every effort to find and apprehend Blee, and at last met with success. Blee was taken to Greenwich to be questioned.

It was here that Cox learnt the whole truth of the matter. Blee, it seems, was all too willing to talk. McDaniel and Berry were the ringleaders of a gang of London criminals. Over perhaps twenty years, they had 'earned' over £1,720 from turning in others to the law, which had resulted in over 100 people being convicted. On each occasion, they had engineered a fraudulent conviction of a man known to be innocent and had duly claimed the reward money for his apprehension. On one occasion, the two victims explained how they had been seduced by the gang, but the thief takers' evidence was too strong and they were hanged. But by early July 1755, the money had dried up and they needed a fresh victim. Blee, who lodged with Berry as his servant, was asked, 'Tom, money grows scarce, you must give a sharp look out for a couple to go upon the scamp now, and if you can't get two, you must get one.' Blee also claimed that his life was in danger, 'McDaniel once got a long knife and threatened to cut my throat.'

In the mean time, plans were hatched at two pubs, Sir John Oldcastle's and the Bell inn, at Holborn. They decided that the 'robbery' would take place at Deptford because that was where most rewards would be obtained, as has been noted. Salmon would make some breeches and include an identifying mark on them. Other possessions would have similar marks, so there could be no doubt that, when the thieves were apprehended, the goods could be identified as having been stolen.

Blee was given money by Berry to find a couple of likely lads and ply them with drink before suggesting the theft to them. Picking two petty criminals, he found the work easy. For the next fortnight he stayed in their company, buying them cheap gin and ensuring that they would be ready for the work as suggested. There was no problem in this.

As to the actual execution of the plan, Blee also stayed in close contact with the others, and especially Salmon, to ensure that he would be in the right place at the right time. Salmon played his part admirably, and after the 'theft' Berry and Blee arranged matters so that Egan, then McDaniel, could come into the picture and engineer the arrest. They thought that their plan had succeeded and the spoils were theirs for the taking. However, Cox's work, *caused them all to be apprehended, and the one moment they found themselves involved in the same calamity which they had rejoiced to bring upon others. They were now seized with consternation and terror.*

Kelly and Ellis were presumably then set free (they are certainly not heard of again in the court records) whilst the four conspirators were tried at Maidstone on 13 August on the grounds that they had employed Kelly and Ellis to commit a robbery. Although they were discharged, they were sent to London for trial.

This took place at the Old Bailey in February of the following year. Here they were charged with being accessories to the robbery before the act took place. The four claimed they were all entirely innocent. Egan and Berry said they had never been to the Bell; Salmon that he had been at home throughout and McDaniel said of Blee's statement, 'He mentioned that he had been four or five times up in Holborn, I never was there with him in my life.' Although Blee's testimony against them was sufficient to convict them all, a couple of other men stated that they had seen the gang together in recent times.

The Gentleman's Magazine indulged in some moralizing over the matter,

Of these wretches, and of the projection, progress and execution of the scheme which has been lately discovered, a particular account should be transmitted for posterity, as a singular instance of the perversion of human laws, and the astonishing degradation of human nature by habitual wickedness.

The discovery of the conspiracy was due to astute work on the part of Cox. Had it not been for him, a great miscarriage of justice would have taken place. Yet this exposure of thief takers as criminals did not bring about reforms to the system. After all, to create a permanent salaried force of professionals would be expensive as well as potentially oppressive. Englishmen valued their liberties as well as their wallets and, if abuses occurred, they had to be borne. Yet a system which relied on thief takers and rewards for the capture of criminals promoted the very crimes the law was meant to suppress, and this affair had been a prime example of this.

However, it was difficult to know with what offence the four be prosecuted. A panel of special judges had to be convened in order to come to a decision. It was only under the Forgery Act of 1727 that they could be prosecuted. This offence carried seven years in prison and two sessions in the pillory. After the seven-year gaol sentence expired, each man had to find bail of £1,000 each – an impossible sum and tantamount to life imprisonment, which *The Newgate Calendar* said was 'well suited to such mischievous, hard hearted and unrelenting villains'. This was to prove as fatal as if they had been taken to the gallows.

At noon on 5 March 1756, McDaniel and Berry were put in the pillory at the end of Hatton Garden and were 'severely treated by the populace that their lives were supposed to be in danger'. Apparently 'such a Multitude of People was never known to be assembled on such an Occasion'. Other criminals were severely dealt with – two pickpockets were apprehended and 'were so severely disciplined by the populace, that they were scarce able to crawl away'. Salmon and Egan, who were placed in the middle of Smithfield three days later, had an even worse fate. According to *The Newgate Calendar*, as soon as the mob saw them exposed there,

> *they pelted them with stones, brickbats, potatoes, dead dogs and cats and other things. The constables now interposed, but being soon over-powered, the offenders were left wholly to the mercy of an enraged mob. The blows they received occasioned their heads to swell to a monstrous size and by people hanging to the skirts of their clothes, they were nearly strangled. They had been in the pillory about half an hour when a stone struck Egan on the head and he immediately expired.*

The sheriffs feared that if the others were once again exposed to 'popular justice' they would be killed, so they were not put in the pillory again. In April, Berry was tried, alongside Mary Jones, a prostitute, with the murder of one Joshua Kidden, who had been falsely convicted of robbery in the previous year. However, the two were discharged due to lack of evidence.

This did not help Berry much. He and his two surviving con-federates all died soon after in the unhealthy confines of Newgate Prison. A fitting punishment indeed.

CHAPTER 5

The Deptford Jacobite Conspiracy
1757

May God bless King James and Prince Charles, you know who I mean ...

Since the expulsion of James II from the throne in 1688, his descendants had tried to regain the crown he had lost. Their supporters were known as Jacobites from the Latin Jacobus for James. There were a number of rebellions in their favour and foreign powers had often been invited to invade in order to restore the Stuarts. The battle of Culloden, near Inverness, in 1746, was a decisive defeat to the Jacobite cause, but it did not put an end to schemes to place James's son, James Francis Stuart, on the throne as James III. A restoration seemed possible once Britain and France were at war in what was to be known the Seven Years War (1756–63). After all, if France managed to plant a Stuart on the throne, then they could hope for an amicable settlement with their virulent enemy.

Maritime supremacy was of the essence for both Britain and France. If France could defeat Britain at sea, then an invasion was possible. This required information, which could be provided by those Englishmen who were eager to restore the Stuarts. Of these, only a minority were prepared to take any action and the British Government took steps to prevent such conspiracies succeeding.

On 17 July 1756, the Commissioners for the Excise – a key department of state – gave the following instruction to their officers:

> *if they shall discover or be informed of any hostile preparations to land on the coasts of Sussex, Essex, Kent, Hants or Dorset, or shall suspect any persons to be assisting such a Design to send immediate intelligence thereof to the commanding officers of His Majesty's forces in these counties.*

Henry Page, gentleman and excise officer of Deptford, was doubtless mindful of this instruction when he overheard the following

Deptford Royal Dockyard. London Borough of Lewisham

snatch of conversation at the Bell alehouse, 'this is a plan of the Navy and this is a list of the Land Forces and as soon as I get a plan of Portsmouth and Chatham, I will go over to France with them'. Page did not see the speaker, but he thought he might be one William Dunster, a local tailor who was originally from Wiltshire. Page told his superior, Mr Gauldicott, who told him to investigate the matter.

Page was to join Dunster's band and find out what he could. This turned out to be fairly easy as the amateur plotters did not regard secrecy as important. Page met Dunster in an alehouse and whilst there heard singing in the street, 'Over the water to Charley'. This was a reference to Charles Edward Stuart, James Stuart's son and known to some as Bonnie Prince Charlie. Dunster asked Page if he agreed with such sentiments and Page claimed he did.

Thinking he had found a fellow Jacobite, Dunster took Page into his own house. Here he showed him the lists which he had previously talked about to others. Dunster boasted that the French authorities would pay him £500 for such information. But there was as much conviviality as conspiracy with the Deptford Jacobites. Page heard

Jacobite toasts made openly in the Jolly Sailor, He even observed a 'secret' oath-taking ceremony. Here, Dunster joined hands with one Richard Whittick, a labourer, and they made the following toast, 'May God bless King James and Prince Charles, you know who I mean him who is called the Pretender, and not that old blackguard, George.' Page also later claimed that Whittick and Dunster pledged to join any French invasion of England.

In early August, Dunster began to become more active. He went to Portsmouth, which was a key naval base, in order to stay with Thomas Tiggins, a shoemaker. Helpfully, Page encouraged him to make the visit and paid his travel expenses. It was here that plans and sketches of the fortifications had been made. The Jacobites' next challenge was how to remit to France the information they had assembled. One answer was to employ Mrs McCullock of Wapping, whose husband was in the French army. This plan was not adopted. Instead, they chose Archibald Manson, another Deptford Jacobite, who was staying at Dunster's and had served in the French army in the previous decade. He had the plans sewn into his coat and, for a guinea and a half, was to meet two Dutch sailors at Tower Hill and to make the exchange there.

The exchange never took place. Acting on information given by Page, one Carrington, who may have been a King's Messenger, arrested the gang members. Dunster and Manson were taken when they were about to embark for Ostend. Now the wheels of the judicial machine began to grind. Evidence was taken from Page and Alex McGraw, a journeyman tailor in Dunster's employ. Manson told his questioners that Dunster talked of going to Scotland and wanted him to take an oath to say he would join any French invasion. Dunster admitted that he administered the oath which Page had witnessed and that he had visited Tiggins. But he denied he was planning to go to France.

The Jacobites – Whittick, McGraw and another, one McQuill, a labourer – were sent to Maidstone gaol to await the next Assizes. Why there was no mention of Dunster is a mystery. After all, he seems to have been the ringleader. Did he escape, or turn King's evidence? The former seems likely, as if it had been the latter, he would have been needed for the trial.

McQuill and Whittick were, eventually, the only two to stand trial, and this was at Rochester at the Lent Assizes in 1758. But they were not charged with being involved in a treasonable plan, but with a lesser, and more easily proved, offence, that of making seditious toasts, as witnessed by Page. The official indictment read that they did

most unlawfully, wickedly and maliciously devising . . . to molest . . .
the happy state and publick peace . . . falsely and audaciously to insin-
uate and make it believed and thought of as if . . . the King . . . had no
right or title . . . to the Crown.

Even worse, they had said these seditious words in public, 'with a loud
voice and in a publick open and audacious manner these wicked
scandalous seditious and malicious English words'. The court
deemed the men to be 'wicked seditious malicious and ill disposed'.

The sentence was fairly minor, especially during wartime – a
nominal fine of a shilling each and three months in gaol. It is also
noteworthy that the authorities still believed that Jacobitism was a
political danger to the state, and that there were men who were sympathetic towards the Stuart cause. There was a real danger of a French
invasion throughout the early years of the Seven Years War. The
threat was only at an end when the French fleets were smashed by the
Royal Navy at Lagos and Quiberon Bay in 1759. With the accession
of George III, who 'glorified in the name of Britain' in the following
year, the appeal of Jacobitism spiralled further down.

CHAPTER 6

Death of a Customs Officer 1776

Damn his eyes, he has not got enough, let us go back and beat him some more ...

Smugglers, as with pirates, have a romantic aura for those who are not threatened by them. Some respectable contemporaries, including Sir Robert Walpole, leading minister under the first two Georges, and his fellow Norfolk resident, the Revd James Woodforde, bought drink from them. Goods such as tea, chocolate, brandy and tobacco were liable to high customs duties, and so smuggled goods would be cheaper as they were untaxed – yet the smugglers, of course, still made a profit. Only the government lost money. But smugglers were often violent criminals as much as 'free traders' and smuggling was certainly not a 'victimless crime'. Certainly the officers of the law could be in great danger. Often the army had to be summoned to combat smuggling gangs. Mr Charles, an excise man, was shot dead in Lewisham in 1736 and, as we shall see, another lost his life later in the century.

The Thames-side town of Deptford was an important dockyard. Customs and Excise men waged a constant war with the smuggling gangs. On 10 April 1776, the customs men received a tip off that 'a quantity of tea was to be run in the night'. Therefore, four officers, Joseph Pierson, William Anchor, Richard Burr and William Bacon, armed themselves with pistols and at eleven o'clock at night set off to the turnpike road which ran from Deptford to Blackheath. Here they waited for the smugglers. Anchor later recalled:

we waited there some time; then we saw two men come down the road which reaches from Blackheath to the turnpike; it was then near twelve o'clock; these two men seemed to be in liquor; they ran against Mr Pierson and me, and said, How many are there of you?

It was now between eleven and twelve o'clock. In retrospect, it is probable that the tip off was a mere ruse in which to lure the customs men into an ambush, and the two men who appeared to be drunk were acting as spies, ascertaining their enemies' strength. The two men left and gave a loud whistle as they did so. The customs men went towards Blackheath, hoping to catch the smugglers with their goods, but failed to encounter any. So they went back towards Deptford.

As they waited for about twenty minutes, near some elm trees, a group of ten or a dozen men coming from Blackheath, walked past them. They were unarmed and walked up Church Street. A watchman identified them as riggers from Woolwich Yard. However, two of the newcomers stayed behind and watched the customs men, and when being asked what they were doing said it was none of their business. Twenty minutes later, the situation became threatening, as another group of about twelve to fourteen appeared. They wore white frock coats and their hat flaps were pulled low over their faces to conceal their identities. They were armed with sticks and bludgeons. One shouted at the customs men, 'Bugger them, here they are.'

Bacon was the first customs man to be assaulted and was knocked unconscious. The others tried to make a run for it. Burr was also knocked down. Bacon and Pierson were surrounded by three or four of their assailants. They said that they would shoot if they were molested further, but Anchor later claimed they were unwilling to do so – it could have led to them being charged with murder at a future date if they had killed anyone. Their foes were undeterred. One said, 'Blast you, ye dogs, we will sacrifice you.' Six of their confederates soon joined them.

Anchor and Pierson decided to flee. They could not see their other colleagues at this point. The two men ran down Church Street and were pursued. Anchor fell against the chain at Trinity almshouses and was struck a blow under the chin by one of the pursuers. Others ran after Pierson. Anchor disentangled himself and kept on running, following Pierson and rejoining him on Deptford Green. They decided to separate again; with Pierson running towards Hughes' Fields while Anchor carried on along the Green. The time was about half past two.

Three men followed Pierson. They must have caught up with him, for, though he could not see him because of the dark, Anchor heard him cry out, 'O dear'. If recorded correctly, this was a surprisingly mild expression for a man who had just been bludgeoned.

Anchor escaped, but did not see Pierson again until about half past four. The latter was at this time being put into a boat on the Thames. An hour later, both men were in London Hospital. Pierson had been 'violently wounded'. There were 'many cuts upon his head'. Mr Dickerson, the surveyor of Deptford, had had him dressed by John

Trinity Almshouses, Church Street, 1841. London Borough of Lewisham

Franks, a Deptford surgeon. At the hospital, Mr George Nealson examined him and noted the extent of his injuries:

> *he had three or four very dreadful wounds upon his head; he was very badly bruised upon his breast, in short there was not a free place but what was beat and bruised in a very bad manner . . . he was so bruised that he could not stir himself the least in the world: his head, the os frontis, the forehead was laid bare, the occipitis was cut, his breast was dreadful, his right arm was so bruised that we laid it open, there was a large extravasion of blood daily.*

Pierson died of his injuries on 10 May; his wife had been at his bedside throughout.

Three men were arrested: Joseph Blann, Benjamin Harley and Thomas Henman. Their confederates had fled.

At the trial at the Old Bailey, on 22 May, Anchor was the first witness. He said he could not positively identify any of the three prisoners, though he thought he recognized Henman as one of them. Before dying, Pierson had said that he was wearing a frock coat, but that he kept his head down on the night of the affray, so he could not be certain it was Henman. Anchor acknowledged that he did not actually see Pierson being attacked. Bacon, however, said that his assailants were similar to the prisoners in their costume, but once again, could not swear positively, because it had been dark and because their attackers had pulled their hat flaps over their faces. Henman and Harley might have been among the group, but he was uncertain. Burr agreed with this statement and had nothing to add.

Samuel Whiting was the next witness. He had been among the attackers and so had presumably turned King's evidence to save his life from what was a hanging offence. He said that his friends included Gypsey George, said to be a gentleman and the ring leader of the gang, who had escaped arrest, Edward George, Thomas Henman, Robert Harley and Benjamin Harley.

He recalled going to the King's Head in Deptford where he met the rest of the gang. After drinking gin, they went in search of the customs officers. At first this was fruitless. Then, later that night, they split into two parties and searched Blackheath and Greenwich for them. They eventually found the four men. They then all returned to Deptford and kept two men behind so as to keep an eye on the customs men while the others acquired weapons. Gypsey George remarked, 'There are enough of us now to lick them.'

Deptford Green and St Nicholas's Church, 1890s. London Borough of Lewisham

Hughes' Fields, Deptford, c.1840. London Borough of Lewisham

The armed gang then came down Church Street and Gypsey George was at their head. He knocked down Bacon. After that, there was a wild chase. Whiting recalled the scene when they caught up with Pierson:

> *I saw Gypsey George take down Hughes' Fields when he came down to the bottom of Hughes' fields, he seized Pierson by the collar, and said, if he did not tell his name, he would cut his throat.*

The two Harley brothers, Edward George and Whiting were with their leader at this point. Pierson was knocked to the ground and they began to beat him. He begged for mercy and told them he had a wife and four small children. This made no difference to his attackers; as their leader said, 'Damn his eyes, he has not got enough, let us go back and beat him some more.' Pierson received 'several violent blows' to add to those he had already had inflicted upon him.

The Harley brothers begged their leader to desist, though Henman remained silent. Gypsey George took no notice of them, 'Come up, my men, and hit him a blow a-piece for me.' Johnson and Henman inflicted two head wounds apiece on the stricken man. But no one else hit him again, with Pierson begging for mercy. The men then went back to Church Street and to Gypsey George's house in Mill Lane. Here they drank gin and Gypsey George paid his followers a few shillings apiece.

In court, Henman and Harley protested their innocence.

John Dicey was the next witness. He was a waterman from Deptford. He had heard the commotion in the night and got out of bed to investigate. He saw Pierson being attacked and begging for his life. He thought there were three or four attackers, but was not certain. Once the attackers had gone, Dicey went to see if he could help. He recalled, 'he was most terribly beat, and all over blood'. Others came to Pierson's aid, Mr Mitchell, a publican, and John Wright, and between them they conveyed Pierson to Mr Dickerson the surveyor – they had previously asked Franks for help, but had, surprisingly, been refused. Dickerson then ordered Franks to assist and eventually he did so, noting 'four terrible large wounds to the head'. He also noted that there were wounds on Pierson's limbs, too. Dicey also collected Pierson's pistol, which he had dropped in the street. Pierson was asked why he did not shoot and said he was reluctant to kill, even at the expense of his own life. Unfortunately, Dicey could not swear to the identity of Pierson's assailants.

Another witness was Barbara Dudley, of Hughes' Fields, but she could not identify any of the men. A better witness was James Greenrod, a coal porter, who with John Rolfe had met the gang just after the attack, as they were on their way home after work. He had recognized Gypsey George, Whiting, the Harley brothers, Edward George and Henman. They were all armed with sticks. Rolfe said the time was between three and four o'clock. He said he and Greenrod had gone with the other men for gin, after having met them and that Gypsey George was paying off his men, as Whiting had already said.

The final evidence came from the deposition made by Pierson to John Sherwood and William Blackmore, London magistrates. He had little to add, except to confirm statements made by previous witnesses and to state explicitly that the attack made on him and his colleagues had been made 'without any provocation whatever'.

It was now time for the prisoners to make their defence. Harley and Henman swore that they were both at home and asleep during the time of the attack. Amelia Toam of Deptford, needlewoman, lived in the same house as Harley and was possibly his mistress. She said that he was there before midnight but, under cross-examination, said she was uncertain that this was the night of the murder. Mrs Ann Hatton, a gardener of Deptford, believed Harley to 'be a very sober honest man, as far as I know', and, crucially, returned home before midnight of the night in question. Other witnesses claimed that it was Gypsey George who was the principal in the attack and that Harley had pleaded that mercy be shown to Pierson. Hannah Campbell of Church Street, with whom Henman lodged, said he was home by two. Other witnesses said that Whiting had told Henman and Harley shortly after their arrest and initial incarceration in the Deptford Cage, 'never mind lads, God almighty will send you out of your trouble, you are both innocent'.

However, the court found Blann not guilty, but sentenced Henman and Harley to death. The prosecution were dependent on Whiting's testimony to reach their verdict and the jury evidently agreed with them, and decided to disregard the testimony of the likes of Amelia Toam, Ann Hatton and Hannah Campbell. The two were executed at Tyburn on 27 May. Their bodies, once cut down, were given to the surgeons for medical research, as was customary practice.

The story continued later that year, as more of the miscreants were caught. On 17 July, at a public house in Bow Street, Robert Harley and Edward George were brought before Sir John Fielding and other magistrates, charged with the killing. Due to evidence given by John Rose and James Greenwood, they were committed to Newgate to stand trial. The trial occurred on 11 September. Samuel Whiting was a principal witness for the prosecution as before. Both men attested to their innocence, Harley claiming,

> *I never was at such a place as this is my life; I am very innocent of what I am charged; I hope the jury will consider of it before they take an innocent life away.*

Sarah Bassett said George was 'a very honest labouring man' and Sarah Hawkins said Harley was 'a very honest good natured man'. Yet despite all this both were found guilty, hanged and their bodies were given over to dissection. The final trial for anyone who was concerned in the killing of Pierson was one George Palmester on 15 January 1777 but, as no evidence was produced against him, he was found not guilty. The principal criminal, Gypsey George, meanwhile, escaped the net. How and why this was so is unknown; it may have been because communication between law officers was poor.

CHAPTER 7

The Blackheath Swindler 1800

She has derived no permanent advantage from her frauds ...

There was national interest shown towards one Miss Eliza Robertson at the turn of the nineteenth century; in part because of her sex. Miss Robertson was born in Bermondsey in about 1771. She was described as being 'plain, much marked by small-pox, about five feet two inches in height, and insinuating in manner'. Initially she earned her living as a teacher in Richmond in the late 1780s. Her father could not aid her as he was greatly in debt. She left London in 1790, and it is unclear whether she was then in Scotland, Ireland or Cheshire. It is possible she was employed by the Cunningham family in Scotland as a governess. It is also conceivable that her stay in Scotland provided her with a germ of an idea which she was later to employ for her own benefit.

From 1795, she ran a boarding school on Croom's Hill, Greenwich. She ran this school with her good friend, Miss Charlotte Sharp, about whom very little is known. Miss Robertson later wrote 'We soon became attracted to each other' and 'I was very happy with Miss Sharp'. What exactly this association between the two spinsters was is unclear. They may have been 'just good friends', or they may have been more intimate, as was suggested by their enemies.

She represented herself as an heiress who would inherit £10,000 and in May 1800 told William Creasy of Greenwich that her uncle, Alexander Stuart Robertson of Fascally, Scotland, was dead. She begged him to accompany her to a lawyer, in order to arrange matters so she might

Miss Eliza Robertson, 1802. London Borough of Lewisham

inherit the property. Believing her word, Creasey lent her £2,000 to tide her over financially until she took possession of what would be hers. Needless to say, Miss Robertson's expectations were wholly fictional.

Miss Robertson now decided to take 3 The Paragon on the southern side of Blackheath. This was in an unfinished state, so she engaged bricklayers, carpenters, painters and other craftsmen 'to finish the premises in the most expensive style'. Whilst the builders were at work, Miss Robertson acquired three carriages and at the end of June set off for the fashionable watering hole of Brighton in style – in a coach with four horses and outriders.

On her return, she continued to order goods on credit. Hatchett's were commissioned to make her an even more elegant carriage, with silver mouldings and raised silver coronets. She had to do this as she said that she would be attending the Queen's birthday, to whom her alleged cousin, Henry Dundas, the Home Secretary, was to introduce her.

Meanwhile, no expense was spared on her Blackheath residence. Mr Oakley of Bond Street, London, was to be in charge of the furnishings, to the tune of £4,000 and he gave her a year's credit. According to *The Gentleman's Magazine*:

> *Things then went on swimmingly: the drawing-rooms were painted in water colours, the walls in landscape. The looking glasses came to £1,100; the principal bed was £500 and every other article was equally magnificent.*

However, Oakley asked for a part payment for all this work, to the tune of £1,000. At which request, Miss Robertson became very annoyed and hurt. She told Oakley that if he had any doubts about her financial probity, then he should apply to her sister Lady Paget, her cousin the bishop of London or to Sir Richard Hill. Oakley was duly impressed by Miss Robertson's alleged relations, and so he said he could wait until the money from the Fascally estate arrived.

However, when the work was almost finished, the creditors were becoming suspicious and they held a meeting on January 1801 at a coffee house at Ludgate Hill, to discuss what to do next. In the following month, Oakley found out the truth. He called upon Sir Richard and then the bishop, and they told him 'they had no further knowledge of Miss Robertson than by a card, which a person of that name had been in the habit of leaving at the houses of persons of distinction'. Oakley then applied to the law and took out a writ for her arrest.

Oakley, together with some of his employees and (probably) some of the Bow Street Runners, went down to The Paragon. Here they

The Paragon, Blackheath, 1864. London Borough of Lewisham

waited for her carriage to return, which it did by nine o'clock in the evening, but she was not in it, because she had received news that they might be waiting there for her and had decided never to return. Then they entered the house by allegedly stating that they were to deliver a carpet, and removed the furniture which she had had installed there. The remaining goods in the house were sold by auction on the following day. Some of the items which were sold belonged to Miss Robertson, as opposed to those which had been obtained from Oakley and others on credit.

It was estimated that Miss Robertson had defrauded numerous tradesmen out of the colossal total sum of £20,000, though one estimate put it at £15,000, 'expended in show and present expense'.

Apart from being a swindler, Miss Robertson was under attack for another reason. *The Gentleman's Magazine* reported, in shocked tones:

> *Mr Pearce, of St Paul's Churchyard, met her last week in Bishopsgate Street, dressed in man's cloaths and boots, with a Miss Sharp leaning on her arm. This female Proteus attended several Presbyterian and other meetings.*

It was not unknown for women to wear men's clothing. Some women (a very few) joined the armed forces, in disguise, and marched and fought in uniform. But it was extremely rare and frowned upon. Miss Robertson was termed 'the lady in men's clothes' and 'the gentleman in ladies' clothes' and these were intended as insults. However, Miss Sharp 'denied most positively that neither her nor Miss R. ever were dressed in men's clothes'. It was thought this was most unwomanly of them.

But where was Miss Robertson? At the end of March 1801, she was apprehended in Huntingdonshire and taken back to London. Here she was examined at Bow Street on 3 April and taken to Newgate. *The Times* noted, 'She has derived no permanent advantage from her frauds. She is represented to be in the greatest distress and entirely destitute of money.' She was finally removed to the debtors' prison, the Fleet. Of her stay here, she later wrote:

I must say this place is well constructed for the convenience of the prisoners: it is very large. The rooms are a good size, and if the people are cleanly, may be made both decent and comfortable . . . [but] . . . it is very injurious to the health to be confined to one room. I have severally felt the effects having been seriously ill.

In July 1802, a Scottish gentleman who arrived in London declared 'that the pretensions of the celebrated Miss Robertson to the estate of Fascally have excited no little surprise in the Highlands of Scotland, at whatever London folks will believe'.

He explained that the estate of Fascally belonged to the family of Strowan, a very ancient name, and was designated as a barony by a royal charter for the younger branch of the family. However, this was on the understanding that if there were no male heirs, it would revert to the older branch. But since the last baronet had been a supporter of the Jacobite cause in 1745, it was forfeited and the heirs could not lay claim to it. In any case, the barony was encumbered with debt and was sold to meet the demands of the creditors. He also stated that Miss Robertson was not a member of the family who had owned the barony and he remained incredulous that people in London believed her claims to wealth.

Miss Robertson was adamant that she was in the right. In her *Memoirs*, she wrote:

I paid such of the tradesmen as had produced their bills . . . They all greatly exceeded their time and orders: and when their conduct is impartially considered, I think they deserve no pity, let their loss be what it may.

In the following year, Miss Robertson hit back at her creditors and brought an action against Oakley and others at the Maidstone Assizes, on the grounds that they had stolen articles of her property from The

Paragon when they removed the furniture from there in the previous year. Mr Garrow was the prosecutor, and argued that the tradesmen had taken illegal liberties in order to secure Miss Robertson's property. He said that any 'ordinary, dull, stupid, honest tradesman' would have had her arrested and sent for trial, instead of seizing her goods and chattels. Miss Sharp appeared as a witness in Miss Robertson's favour. They were countered by the defending counsel who claimed that the prosecutor had been deluded by the artful Miss Robertson, who had duped stone masons, carpenters and upholsterers of late. He also produced a letter from Miss Robertson to say that Oakley was fully justified in removing any of his property from the house. The judge saw this evidence and then threw the prosecution's case out of court.

Miss Robertson wrote a number of tediously self-justifying pamphlets to show that she was in the right and the creditors were the real criminals. They made her some money (about £120) and so her stay in the Fleet was not as uncomfortable as it would otherwise have been. But they had no long-term benefit, for she remained in gaol for the rest of her life and died in the Fleet in June 1805, being buried in St Bride's churchyard as the woman 'of swindling notoriety'.

Before then, Miss Robertson had resigned herself to her fate, writing, 'I trust I shall be endued with resignation to the will of Him who does nothing in vain, and who will finally display everything that may now be enveloped'.

It is hard to know whether to be more surprised by the credulity of Miss Robertson's creditors or her sheer gall and effrontery. She had enjoyed a brief success, but it had been transitory; her downfall was equally swift and her demise followed relatively shortly. Her creditors had been easily taken in by her charm and nerve, impressed by her claims to wealth and her alleged friends in high places. A cautionary tale for all parties.

CHAPTER 8

Murder in Lewisham 1822

I am shot! I am shot through the chest!

At three o'clock in the morning of Sunday 22 December 1822, a shot rang out at a house in Morden Hill, Blackheath. It was heard by Thomas Hawley, a local watchman, who had been standing in his watch booth at Dartmouth Row, 130 yards from the house. Yet he did nothing more for ten minutes, because of his concern that he might be shot if he arrived on the scene whilst the miscreant(s) remained. When a young servant, Robert Papworth, arrived and told him that his master, James Smith, had been shot, he had little alternative to follow the lad to the house.

He was admitted by a maid servant who was understandably 'much agitated'. The delay in his arrival certainly meant that he managed to avoid meeting any suspicious characters. Once there, his uses were limited. What was obviously needed was medical attention. Mr Clement Rose, a surgeon of Cold Bath Row, Greenwich, came to Smith's aid. He initially had been told that Smith had shot himself. When he saw Smith, he was lying on the bed and told the surgeon that he had been shot by would-be burglars. Rose found a gunshot wound in Smith's left arm. His patient was in a poor state. Rose also later noted: 'The deceased mentioned the name of Coleman the whole of the night.' Rose added that Smith did not directly say that Coleman had shot him, but when Rose asked him whom he suspected: 'His answer was "Coleman". He mentioned no other name.'

The Bow Street Runners were alerted a few hours later. Ruthven, one of their principal officers, spent most of that day and night in trying to track down the perpetrators, but without initial success. It was assumed that the gang were experienced London thieves who had come into the countryside in order to burgle houses there.

Smith died on 28 December. An inquest was held at the Green Man Tavern, Blackheath, two days later. Mr Carttar was the coroner and the jury was made up of 'twelve respectable inhabitants'. Witnesses were questioned.

Dartmouth Row, c.1905. London Borough of Lewisham

From them, an account of the events of the early hours of Sunday morning was reconstructed. Apparently, a gang of burglars had attempted to gain entry into the house by boring a hole through one of the square panels in the front door, in order to loosen the fastenings inside. The task had been three-quarters complete. Whilst Smith, who was a heavy sleeper, did not hear what was happening, his wife who was sleeping in the same room did. She woke her husband and told him of her suspicions. He put on his coat and went to an adjacent room, where he threw open the chamber window and called out, 'Who's there? What are you about?'

Scarcely had he uttered these words than one of the burglars pulled out his pistol and fired at him. The shot was accurate and the ball passed through the fleshy part of Smith's arm and entered his chest, lodging between his ribs. Smith screamed and said, 'I am shot! I am shot through the chest!' The would-be burglars then took to their heels. The household was also alerted by the noise. Smith was soon found, covered in his own blood and apparently dead. Yet, as noted, death was not immediate; medical assistance was soon to arrive, but the surgeons did not think the old man could live for much longer. However, Smith was able to say that he had seen two assailants and that one was wearing a salt and pepper coat. Papworth recalled that he saw someone lurking outside and called out to them, but the man disappeared.

When Hawley was questioned the court decided that his behaviour had been discreditable and that he would be soon discharged from his post. When Rose talked about Coleman, the coroner was concerned that such a statement should be made in the court, that a statement not be made against an individual without their being present. Yet one juror disagreed, believing that any relevant information should be heard. So Rose related his information. The jury found that Smith had been murdered by person or persons unknown. A reward of £100 had been initially announced, but it was soon increased to £300.

Coleman had, in fact, been arrested shortly after the murder. He was a blacksmith by trade and 'a most notorious character'. The main evidence against him, however, was not his character, but that he had been seen with a centre-bit and stick in Lewisham shortly before the crime occurred. Later that night he was seen drinking in the Black Horse in Rushey Green, two miles from Smith's house. Apparently, 'His account of himself when he was apprehended was given in such a questionable manner, that the Magistrate ordered him to be remanded.'

The prisoner gave his account of events. On the evening of the killing, he was at the Black Horse from nine o'clock, then left at midnight and walked to the Bull and Butcher on King Street, Deptford,

The Rising Sun, Rushey Green, c.1840. London Borough of Lewisham

arriving at one o'clock on the following morning. He then stayed the
night there. He claimed he carried a centre-bit from one pub to the
other.

Evidence from various witnesses contradicted parts of his statement. One man said that the centre-bit produced by Coleman (a
black and grubby instrument) was not that which he had had in the
first pub – the latter resembling the one found at the scene of the
crime. The other centre-bit was bright and new. Another witness
thought the bit was similar to the one he was offered for sale by
Coleman in the pub. A number of files, as well as the centre-bit,
had been stolen from Mr Buckland's carpenter's shop in Deptford
recently, and some of these tools were given by Coleman to his landlord in lieu of the rent he owed him. A witness at the Deptford pub
who knew Coleman did not recall that he slept there when he said he
had done. All in all, it seemed fairly certain that Coleman was a
burglar who was short of money and took part in the attempted
robbery which led to murder. On 6 January, he was committed at
Maidstone Gaol for trial. Yet Coleman said that he was but one of a
gang of seven who tried to break in, and that he did not fire the fatal
shot. In fact, he claimed it had been fired by one Robert Smith, a
nephew of the deceased.

Coleman was not the only one of the gang to be arrested. With a
reward of £300 posted for the capture of the criminals, some of his
confederates were not at liberty for much longer. On 4 February,
James Smith and Robert Smith (nephews of the deceased) and James
Webster were examined by the Greenwich magistrates. Yet as Mr
Bicknell, Clerk of the Bench observed,

> I have not sufficient evidence to bring home to them the charge of
> murder, and as the entering upon the evidence which I have obtained
> may place other persons, who are suspected, on their guard and prevent
> my eventually convicting them of the crime, I had rather, for the
> present, that the parties should go at large, than that I should enter an
> imperfect case against them.

The chairman of the bench, Richard Smith, agreed, but warned the
three that they were not being discharged because they were innocent.

Shortly after his committal, Coleman requested an interview with
the Blackheath magistrates. They met at the gaol on 9 January.
Coleman told them that he hoped for a royal pardon. He decided
to make a clean breast of it, which overturned his previous story.
Coleman confessed that he was indeed part of the gang which tried to
rob Mr Smith and that he had used the centre-bit in order to try and
effect an entry. Again, he named Robert Smith as the man who had
actually fired the shot.

Coleman was duly tried at the Kent assizes. Mr Andrews, Coleman's advocate, argued that a recommendation for a royal pardon should be made. Yet the prosecuting counsel, Mr Adolphus, argued that this should be ignored. The judge said that royal mercy would be asked for. Coleman did not speak in his own defence. Unfortunately for him, the jury believed him to be guilty of murder and so he was duly sentenced to death. Yet it was widely believed that he would receive mercy.

This was not to be. At Penenden Heath, near Maidstone, Coleman was led forth to the place of execution. He was very contrite and had spent much time in the chaplain's company. The warder was given twelve shillings and a handshake, and Coleman went on his way clasping a prayer book. John Farmer, a Greenwich constable who had accompanied him to Maidstone, asked if he had any messages for anyone and, if so, he would deliver them. Coleman replied: 'No, I have done all that – that is the man I have told you of – Bob is the man'. Yet he did give a yellow silk handkerchief to Farmer:

Take this handkerchief, and give it to a woman named Ann Steel; you know her – tell her I sent it to her – God bless her – don't forget – I hope I am going to a better place.

The chaplain finished his final ministrations and Coleman his last prayers. The hangman was putting the noose around his neck, when Coleman made a final appeal to Farmer:

Robert Smith, that is the man I die for; he is the man that shot his uncle, no other man but him; the Lord forgive me – I am a great sinner, but I am innocent of that – thank God for it – my sins are great his brother James made the bullet, though I did not see him do it his own mouth told me so – God bless you all, everybody.

After he had said a few more words to the hangman, the trap door opened and Coleman died.

This was not the final word on the case. After the execution, suspicion fell on the Timothy brothers. John Timothy was taken in East Smithfield, was examined and sent to Maidstone. Farmer was given a warrant for the arrest of his brother, Thomas. Despite Farmer's best efforts, he could not be found. However, he was brought up before another magistrate on another charge – that of assaulting a young woman. He was taken before the Greenwich magistrates and remanded in custody and soon joined his brother in Maidstone, to await the next Assizes. Webster was also rearrested, though the Smiths seem to have vanished.

On 19 December, there was another trial at Maidstone for the same offence. James Webster, a shipwright, aged thirty-seven, was indicted for the murder of James Smith, now almost exactly one year before. Mr Bolland and Mr Adolphus opened the case for the prosecution. The prime witness was John Timothy, a fisherman of Lambeth. He told the full story of the attempted burglary. The gang met at the Nelson pub in Deptford and consisted of himself, Coleman and James Woodcock, another Lambeth fisherman. The three met at that pub on the night of the burglary. En route to Dartmouth Row, they stopped at a bakehouse, where the rest of the gang, including Webster, were present. Here they prepared for the crime, donning brown paper masks and arming themselves with sticks. Some exchanged hats and jackets so as to conceal their identities further. Robert Smith had a pistol and John Timothy carried the centre-bit.

They arrived at James Smith's house at about midnight. They walked around the house, deciding on the best means of entry. The first obstacles to surmount were the iron railings surrounding the house. Robert Smith was the first man to get over. He thought the best policy was to unlock the gate. As none of them had keys, they broke it open. Once inside, they saw a lighted window. They thought it best to avoid this window, but to enter via a shuttered window elsewhere.

Coleman was trying to open this window with the centre-bit, aided by a confederate. The others were posted around the outside of the house to look out for both anyone rousing inside the house and anyone from the outside who happened to pass by. Time passed and then Timothy heard first a cracking sound, perhaps of wood, followed by a pistol shot. He went to investigate and saw his fellows leaving by the gate. He asked Webster what was going on.

I inquired if the shot had been fired by our party, or a party in the house? Robert Smith said it was he who fired it. I asked why? He said he saw somebody come to the window, and the window rising up; some person was raising up the window where Coleman and my brother were trying to get into the house; and seeing, as he thought, an arm out, he got afraid. He said he just got a glimpse of him, and he was afraid, if he had not fired, that something which he had in his hand would have been thrown down upon them, and would have injured my brother and Coleman.

Then they stood around the house to see what would happen next. When nothing did, they decided to make another attempt at entry. Coleman took the pistol and considered reloading it. Meanwhile, they heard a groan from within the house and thought it best to flee. They ran towards the bakehouse, which was by the river. During their flight, they disposed of their sticks and the pistol was broken up and thrown into the river. After that they all went home.

Timothy explained his motives for explaining what happened:

I came here to confess myself a party to the murder. I know that if I had been tried and convicted, I should have been executed. I am swearing here to save my own life.

He said he was not a thief, as some had said. That was unjust, he claimed. He was merely a look out for others. Thomas Timothy, his brother, was called next, but his version of events was much the same as his brother's.

The jury found Webster guilty of being with the thieving party, but not of the murder. Yet the judge declared that if they thought Webster accompanied the criminals when the killing happened, he was also guilty of murder. The jury then returned, without hesitation, a verdict of guilty. Webster said that he was not guilty of murder. He claimed that the Timothy brothers had concocted the story against him in order to claim the £300 reward money and that it was hard that he was convicted on no evidence whatsoever. The judge said that the evidence of the Timothy brothers had been corroborated by others and so passed the death sentence. Webster was hanged on the following Monday and his body given to the surgeons for dissection.

Since neither Coleman nor Webster fired the fatal shot, it may seem harsh that they were executed for the murder. Robert Smith would seem to have been the man who pulled the trigger and killed James Smith. But by the standards of the time, all of the would-be burglars were collectively guilty of murder because all were present when it occurred, even though they did not fire the fatal shot. It is unknown what happened to Robert Smith. Presumably he managed to escape justice, probably by escaping overseas, whilst his fellows were hanged for it or turned King's evidence. He was a lucky man – unlike two of his companions.

CHAPTER 9

Death to the Police (1) 1839

So help me God, I was not present at the affray on Sunday night ...

Ten years after the introduction of the Metropolitan Police Force, a constable was killed in Deptford. Apparently on 30 September 1839, 'the town of Deptford was thrown into the highest state of excitement in consequence of a policeman, named William Aldridge, No. 204 of the R division, having died at an early hour from the effect of injuries received.'

It all began at about half past five, or a little after, on the evening of Sunday 29 September 1839. PC George Stevens was on his beat on New King Street, Deptford, when he saw John Pine, a woodcutter, noisily wrestling with one Kerry. Pine had just come out of the Navy Arms along with John Calvert, where Mrs Hubble, the landlady, said they had been causing trouble. Although Stevens had been told about this, policemen were not allowed to enter a public house unless there was a serious disturbance there (drunkenness among officers was common). Pine and Kerry were making a noisy disturbance. Stevens advanced towards them and told them to go home quietly as they were disturbing the peace. Pine told Stevens he would be damned before he obeyed. Steven repeated his request and said that, if Pine refused, he would be arrested. Pine said it would take more than eleven men to do that.

Pine and his former combatant then went down Lower Road, followed at a discreet distance by Stevens. They stopped near Timothy Ody's timber yard in the same street. The two men were joined by numerous others. Stevens again addressed Pine and his friend, asking them to go home or he would have to take him to the station house. Pine approached Stevens and struck him, knocking the policeman's hat off. Stevens took Pine by the collar. It was then that Aldridge went to his colleague's aid.

It was a dangerous situation for the two constables; Pine was violent and began to attack the men who were holding him. In consequence of this, Stevens was obliged to strike him. By this time, the mob had

Broomfields, Evelyn Street, eighteenth century. London Borough of Lewisham

grown to about 500 or 600; presumably there was a great hostility towards the police by the working men of the locality. Someone shouted, 'Pitch into the police.'

The policemen drew their staves. They took their prisoner up the road and reached the toll gate. The mob then began to throw stones at them and they lost their hats. Since gas pipes were then being laid in Deptford, there was plenty of material about to be used as missiles. Stevens and Aldridge tried to take shelter in the toll house in order to prevent Pine being rescued. They were beaten to it and told that, if they went inside, the house's windows would be broken. With their backs to the house's outer wall, and feeling very tired, they yet retained their hold on Pine, even though they were still subject to a hail of missiles.

They were joined by another two policemen, Joseph Buckmaster and George Baker, who had been on duty in the High Street and had been told of the commotion by a lad. Despite being molested, they managed to get as far as the Telegraph on Broomfield Place. Pine was still abusive; on Buckmaster's and Baker's approach, he said, 'here is another fat b***, if I had a knife, I would stick him'.

Someone in the mob shouted, 'Give it to that b*** without a hat'. It was then that Aldridge was struck, on the side of his head, before

Gibraltar Toll Gate, Evelyn Street, Deptford, 1841. London Borough of Lewisham

falling to the ground. He put his hand to his head and exclaimed, 'Oh, my poor head.' Once again, this is what was recorded, but doubtless the language used at the time was stronger.

He then fell to the ground, bleeding from the mouth and the back of the neck. He staggered as far as the doorstep of Mrs Betsy White's house, putting his hand to his head before falling. Patrick Sullivan, who was with the mob, then said: 'Give it them, there are only three left.' One John Burke threw a stone at Aldridge and shouted, 'There, you b***; how do you like that?'

At this point evidence about the confrontation comes to an end; perhaps the police received further reinforcements and so their assailants dispersed. In any case, at a quarter past seven, Sergeant McGill was able to enter Mrs White's house on Lower Road. He found Aldridge lying on a carpet, 'with his head streaming with blood and rapidly sinking into a state of insensibility'. McGill asked the badly injured man how he felt, and Aldridge managed to say that he did not feel at all well; briefly described the evening's events before he had been struck on the head and fell unconscious.

Edward Dawning was the surgeon attached to the police. He came along to see what he could do. Aldridge complained of a pain behind the ear, and Dawning found that this was an elliptic laceration. Dawning gave him brandy and suggested Aldridge be taken to hospital. Aldridge refused and asked to be taken home, and was taken to his house in Lee, on a stretcher. Dawning was called at three o'clock in the morning as Aldridge's condition had deteriorated. Aldridge died at about five o'clock. His shirt collar and stock were saturated with blood.

The post-mortem examination was carried out by Mr Carr of Lee Terrace and Mr Hoare of Blackheath. The contusions and fractures to the head were deemed sufficient to have caused death. However, the fatal blow was one on the right side of the head, just under the ear. The inner plate of the skull had been beaten in (Aldridge had had a fairly thin skull), and excessive force must have been used. It could not have been the result of a fall, but of a stone, a stick or a powerful kick.

A number of men were arrested – not only John Pine, but also his brother William Pine, Joseph Pickering, John Williams, Daniel Carey, Thomas Findlay, John Henwright and George Calvert. These men were labourers and all aged in their twenties. They were first taken to the police station on Blackheath Road, and then to the magistrates' office in Deptford High Street.

On 1 October PC Conner went to arrest one William Calvert, against whom there were witnesses, and he found his man at the Sheer Hulk on New King Street. He explained why he was arresting Calvert, who replied 'So help me God, I was not present at the affray on Sunday night' and added that he had witnesses to prove it.

The inquest took place at the Swan Inn, Lee, on 2 October. Many people attended; the long room in which the court was held was described as being 'crowded to suffocation'. There were statements by the surgeons and the three surviving witnesses, not to mention a number of members of the public who had been in Deptford on the evening in question, and all testified to the abusive and violent nature of the mob. One man even congratulated the police on keeping hold of the prisoners in the dangerous situation they had been in.

The question to answer was who was responsible for Aldridge's death. Edward Woolmer of Church Street said that it was William Calvert who threw the fatal stone. Woolmer was emphatic in his statement, adding:

I knew Calvert before, and I am not mistaken in the man, and am positive he threw the stone. There were other stones being thrown at the time. I saw a stone thrown by Calvert and that stone struck deceased while in a stooping position . . . Calvert was not more than a yard from the deceased when he threw the stone.

The Swan, Lee. The author

James Richards, pot boy at the Rodney was another witness and he
recalled Calvert being nearby at the crucial time. Mr Pelham was the
solicitor defending the prisoners and he said that he was there at the
time too and was uncertain whether Calvert threw a stone at Aldridge.
It was noted that there had been many respectable people looking
on as the violence escalated, but though they shouted 'Shame' at
the mob, they did not interfere in any other way. Pine claimed he
had been injured, too, on the night of the incident, but the coroner
evinced no sympathy for him. The inquest was adjourned until
Friday.

When the inquest reconvened, at the same location, all the
prisoners were brought there in handcuffs. Mr Sidery, the foreman of
the jury, had visited the scene of the crime on the previous day and
drew a plan for the benefit of his fellow jurors. A number of additional
Deptford residents came forward as witnesses, but could add nothing
of importance. Inspector Phipps produced a handful of flint stones,
weighing between two ounces and three quarters of a pound, of the
type thrown at his colleagues on Sunday evening.

Ody, the wood dealer, outside whose yard the mob assembled, was
next to speak. He denied knowing any of the prisoners, except Pine,
who were all woodcutters, but it later transpired that he did know
most of them. He claimed he saw no stone throwing, did not attack

any policeman and was only absent from his house for two or three minutes. Stevens however said that Ody was among the mob and helped incite them to violence.

Woolmer was again involved. One James Lewis said that he had not seen Woolmer at the scene, but Woolmer stuck to his previous story. The jury retired to discuss the case with the coroner for half an hour. On their return, they had Ody bound over to appear on 8 October, when the inquest would be reconvened. In the interim, John Burke and William Saltwell were arrested.

There was great local excitement in the drama. When the prisoners were transported to Lee for the next stage of the inquest, an omnibus had to be hired to hold them all. A strong body of police escorted them, watched by 'a large concourse of persons'.

Downing gave the medical evidence. He said that it was impossible to say what object caused the ragged wound. He ruled out a fall and a round stone, but he did say that a 'woodnail' (perhaps a piece of wood with a nail in it) thrown with great force might have caused the type of wound which had killed Aldridge. Stevens said that Calvert had been amongst the mob and had hissed the police. Calvert said he had been asleep in the Globe at the said time. Pelham said that, as the inquest was not a court of law, he did not think it was proper at this stage to bring forward witnesses to speak on behalf of the prisoners.

The coroner then began the summing up to what he said was a very difficult case. Of the forty-two witnesses who had been called to give evidence, only four or five had had anything directly pertinent to say as to who killed Aldridge. The jury then went to discuss the matter and returned with a verdict. They said that death was due to wilful murder by Calvert as the principal and the Pine brothers and Burke were accessories. They also added that they had been very impressed by the behaviour of the police and thought that they had done very well on a most trying occasion.

There was an additional court appearance at Deptford on 11 October for two men who had previously appeared as witnesses but were new prisoners – Ody and one Alfred Courthope, a coach-maker. The two men were identified by witnesses as being among the mob. One tried to speak to Pelham, but was told by Phipps to be quiet, which resulted in Pelham reprimanding him, 'I beg you to not interfere between me and my clients Mr Phipps; this is not a Star Chamber, I believe.'

Courthope complained about his presence, claiming to have been at his lodgings at the Globe when the riot occurred. Emma French, daughter of the toll house keeper, said she saw him there. However her father, though agreeing with her, said that Courthope had not encouraged the mob. The court then decided to discharge him as there was no evidence against him. Courthope told Phipps that he would bring an action against him. The remaining prisoners were then all conveyed to Newgate to await trial. Bail was £50 each – a high sum for men in humble circumstances, but a few of them managed it.

They were brought to trial at the Old Bailey on 24 October. Evidence was given by Mrs Hubble and Stevens against the four principal prisoners. They recounted the information they had spoken of on previous occasions. Others testified that these statements were true. Mr Clarkson, for the defence, said that the offence should not be murder, but one of manslaughter.

The jury then retired to decide their verdict. They had a very unpleasant experience, because the ventilation in the small room in which they had to go to make their decision was so defective that they had to break a hole in the roof in order that they might breathe. It took them an hour to reach their verdict. This was that the prisoners were not guilty of murder, but were guilty of manslaughter. Sentence was deferred to the following day.

On 25 October, the prisoners learnt of their fates. Mr Baron Gurney, the judge addressed them thus:

> you were severally indicted for the crime of murder, and the jury who tried you took a very lenient view of the case in acquitting you of that most serious offence, and finding you guilty of manslaughter of an aggravated description, for I have no hesitation in stating now that the case was as nearly as possible a case of murder.

Pine was thought by Gurney to be the most guilty of all as he began the fracas in the public house, then refused to obey the police, attacked one of them and wished he had been able to knife them. Finally, Pine had encouraged the others to attack the police, which they did, in a most vicious way. Calvert was then named as the man who had actually killed Aldridge, albeit unintentionally. Of lesser gravity were Pine's brother and Burke, though they had taken part in the attacks on the police. This incident should be viewed in the wider light of general hostility among some in the working classes towards the 'new police'

John Pine, who was considered to be the principal culprit, was transported to Australia for the reminder of his natural life. He was sent aboard *The Mangles* ship bound for New South Wales on 21 November 1839. Calvert was also transported, though only for fifteen years, and was sent to Van Diemen's Land on 24 February in the following year. Burke and William Pine were each given two years in gaol, with hard labour. Two others were given four months, one other was given two months and six, including Ody, were given a month in gaol each, for their part in rioting. Gurney hoped that these sentences would deter idle and disorderly persons from taking part in violent riots which resulted in death and danger. The jury were relieved that their task was over (they had been involved in other trials apart from this one). The police were praised for their efficiency and the proper manner in which they had given evidence and had behaved during cross-examination. The 'new police', as some still deemed them, were making progress.

CHAPTER 10

Death to the Police (2) 1846

... there was an Irish row in the alley ...

Hostility to the 'new police' in Deptford was apparent, as has been shown already. But it was also the case that those in authority were not always sympathetic to them either. In 1833, Lord Holland thought that the killing of a constable in a riot in Clerkenwell was justifiable, as did the jurymen on the inquest. The case to be discussed in this chapter is suggestive of similar attitudes.

It should have been an everyday night in Deptford. James Usher, a local greengrocer, was walking homeward along New King Street, after drinking at the Navy Arms, at about 12.25 am on Saturday 21 February 1846. He later recalled that, 'upon proceeding up the above street, when about 160 yards from the [Tinderbox] alley, he heard faint cries of "police"'.

Usher entered the alley and saw a man there. He asked him, 'Hallo, who are you, what do you stand there to frighten people for?' On closer inspection, Usher noted 'the policeman was frightfully wounded in the face, but at that time it was not bleeding much'. Usher could not see anyone else in the vicinity; no one was running away from the scene. So he led the constable to the Noah's Ark, which was nearby, as it was impossible to move him any further. Usher ran down New King Street and found Police Sergeant Welton to accompany him back to the pub.

Here they found the injured man to be 'bleeding profusely'. Welton saw that his injured colleague was PC James Hastie, 'a well conducted man and active in the discharge of his duties' and whom he had last seen at five past twelve. Hastie had joined the police in July 1844 and had been recently appointed to Deptford some months previously. A surgeon was summoned and finally Hastie was taken to Guy's Hospital. The wounds were dangerous – there were a number of cuts and fractures to the skull.

Sergeant Lovell investigated the scene of the crime and found signs of a struggle, together with a pool of blood. There were broken shards

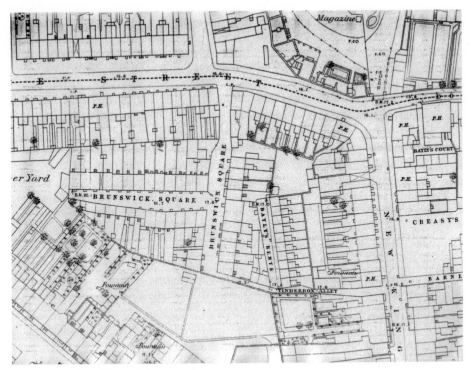

Tinderbox Alley, 1868. London Borough of Lewisham

of a chimney pot nearby too. He traced footsteps leading to Brunswick Square. There were also marks of bloody hands at water closets
belonging to two addresses in the square. William Sullivan, a sawyer,
and William O'Keefe resided there and, though O'Keefe denied all
knowledge of the crime, they were examined. There was blood on
Sullivan's trousers.

Other men were also arrested. These were Cornelius McCarthy
and Michael Collins, both labourers, and, as with the two others,
Irishmen. There were bloodstains on McCarthy's waistcoat, though
one John Dyball said that these were caused when McCarthy helped
him to cut up a pig.

Although Hastie was seriously injured, it was hoped he would
recover once in the hands of Mr Cottingham and the other surgeons.
Yet the various wounds to his head, probably caused by blunt
instruments, were serious indeed. He had intervals of consciousness
and mentioned the names of Sullivan, O'Keefe, McCarthy and
Collins. Likewise, when they were brought before him by Superintendent Mallilieu, his superior, he was able to call them by name.
Later, though, it was argued that Hastie was not in a fit state to be able

to recognize the men before him as being his attackers. Unfortunately, he died on 4 March and the charge against the four men was now one of murder. His funeral was well attended, with 4,000–5,000 people showing their last respects. He was buried at the churchyard of St Paul's Deptford.

The four men mentioned above, along with Timothy Driscoll, a labourer, and William Brosohan, a sawyer, both of Brunswick Square, had been quickly arrested by the police. They were put in Horse-monger Lane Gaol, though Driscoll and Brosohan were soon re-leased. Mr Pelham, who defended them, reminded the jury that they should not let their indignation about the murder prejudice them against the defendants. Mr Payne, the city coroner, began the inquest on 9 March. He heard a number of depositions taken from witnesses.

Between them, the witnesses were able to reconstruct most of what had happened. The first was Henry Brooks, landlord of the Rodney. He recalled that there had been a number of customers in the pub at midnight, including Sullivan, O'Keefe, McCarthy, Collins, Driscoll, William Ford, Thomas Furnivall, Alfred Edwards (these latter three were all dockyard labourers), and Mary Harding, a prostitute. At five minutes past midnight, Brooks asked them to leave the premises and by a quarter past, they had complied.

Brooks did not see what happened next, but he had his ears open, and his former customers remained in the vicinity of the pub. He heard a woman, presumably Mary, screaming – she was being molested by the men around her – and then he heard Hastie's voice. 'Come now my lads, see about getting home, or I shall lock some of you up.'

At this crucial moment, Brooks went to bed, and though he heard some noises for a short time later, he assumed these might have been made by would-be burglars who were trying to break into his cellar. When he found this was not the case, he went to sleep.

Closer to the drama was Mrs Edith Myles, wife of a dock labourer, who lived just off the alley. She said that she heard scuffling and saw a group of men, one was reeling as if drunk, and who said, 'Don't murder me' several times. Mrs Myles minded her own business, shut her door and remarked to her husband, 'There was an Irish row in the alley'.

Henry Brooke, the fishmonger who lived opposite the Rodney, recalled that the group of men took Mary into the alley before he left the scene. Not all of the pub's customers were involved in the attack. Ford left and went home, but not before recalling that some of his fellows had been 'larking' with Hastie. He urged Driscoll to return home, too, the two men lodging under the same roof: 'For God's sake, come home'. Furnivall, Edwards and Mary also went home after Hastie ordered them to depart.

At the inquest, the jury retired at five to discuss their verdict and an hour later returned a unanimous one of wilful murder against the four accused. They would then go before the magistrates' court.

Mr Triall, a newly appointed magistrate, heard the case at Greenwich Magistrates' Court on 9 April. He had to decide whether the four men should be tried at the Old Bailey for the murder of Hastie. Mr Hayward, from the Treasury Solicitor's Office, was leading for the prosecution.

Hayward called the Brosohan family of Brunswick Square, Deptford, where Sullivan and O'Keefe lodged. Peter Brosohan, the householder, said that the two men had returned between midnight and one o'clock on the night of the murder. Sullivan informed him on his return that a row had taken place. His wife added that the row had involved the police and their daughter verified this statement. Sullivan also mentioned that his landlord's poker had been broken – on examination this was found to be untrue. Mallilieu told the court of his colleague's dying declaration. Traill decided to remand the case until 30 April in the hope that new evidence would come to light.

The final examination occurred on 6 May. Hayward called another witness but did not think his testimony would strengthen the case: Jeremiah Lane, a stoker on board HMS *Terrible*, had been lodging at Deptford on the night of the murder. He slept at his uncle's house, his uncle being Brosohan. He had gone to bed at 10.30. Sullivan and O'Keefe returned somewhat later (all three men shared the same room) and Sullivan had awoken Lane to have a brief chat. On the following day, on his way to his ship at Woolwich, there was considerable talk in the streets about the assault and Sullivan's name was mentioned. Had Sullivan spoken to him about it? He had not, replied Lane. This had not, indeed, helped much.

Traill then summed up. According to the report in *The Times*:

> He had very carefully and minutely examined all the evidence, and although there were very strong suspicions as to the guilt of the prisoners, there was not sufficient evidence to send them for trial. The evidence taken altogether, both at the court and before the coroner, only amounted to a case of strong suspicion. Under these circumstances he felt himself bound to discharge the prisoners.

He thought that the coroner's jury had 'no doubt acted from very conscientious motives' and that 'There had been so many persons mixed up in this dreadful affair, that he had no doubt that the guilty party would ultimately be brought to justice'. Hayward said he was not instructed to press for the execution of the coroner's warrant, as the evidence there had not been as detailed as that given at the present hearing. The prisoners bowed to the court and retired, free men.

Reactions were mixed. Some were happy; 'they were cheered by a parcel of women in the street waving handkerchiefs in a token of victory'. Others were very astonished at the result, especially because the coroner's warrant had been withdrawn.

Traill had certainly erred on the side of leniency and clearly gave the four prisoners before him the benefit of the doubt. Perhaps this was due to his inexperience, or perhaps because he was unsympathetic towards the police. It is very probable that he gave the wrong verdict as it seems almost certain that the four were guilty. After all, they were the four men last seen with Hastie, and shortly afterwards he was found badly wounded. It is likely that when the zealous Hastie ordered the crowd home, those who did not obey, perhaps fuelled by alcohol and hostility to the police, decided to attack him and, in doing so, caused him injuries which were to prove fatal.

The postscript to the story is that, in November 1851, one William Cressy was charged with the murder. He had been apprehended by Superintendent Hutton of the Kent County Police and James Baker, parish constable of Peckham. Yet Cressy was discharged by the magistrates because of insufficient proof against him, leaving Hutton and Baker claiming expenses to cover their costs.

CHAPTER 11

A Failed Suicide Bid
1861

She proposed that we should drown ourselves ...

George Inkpen, a twenty-year-old hammerman of Deptford, employed by the General Steam Navigation Company, was described in positive terms by all who knew him, though was also said to be 'a simple-looking youth'. A pivotal (and almost fatal) day in his life was 11 November 1861.

It started ordinarily enough, without any hint of what was to happen and where it would eventually lead him. He had been to a race at Hackney Wick and then returned to Deptford by train, alighting at Deptford High Street. It was here that he parted with a friend,

Deptford High Street and railway station, 1839. London Borough of Lewisham

William Day, and told him they would meet later that evening at ten o'clock at the Ship and Billett, where Day worked as a waiter. He then had a shave by a barber called Bennett. His next port of call was the Lord Duncan pub in New Cross Road. Whilst he was at the bar, Margaret Edmunds, a twenty-four-year-old servant who worked in Florence Road, Deptford, and who had been walking out with Inkpen for the past two years, arrived. According to Inkpen:

> *I went out after her, and we had some conversation, and she asked me to have some of the beer, which I did, and we drank it between us. In the course of further conversation she said it was of no use living, for her friends were always 'nagging' at her. We then walked down the Mornington-road towards the Surrey canal, when we got there she proposed that we should drown ourselves.*

Inkpen seemed not to have raised any objections to entering into what was a suicide pact with his beloved, and made no remark to explain his behaviour nor tried to dissuade Margaret from the steps she was proposing. He was probably quite drunk at the time and promised to go with her wherever she went.

Margaret then asked Inkpen if he had got a handkerchief to tie themselves together with, and he produced one, which she said was too short; not being long enough to tie them both together. She said: 'I have got some tape with me, but I did not bring it out for that

New Cross Road and the Lord Duncan, 1841. London Borough of Lewisham

purpose.' Inkpen then remembered that he had bought some boot laces earlier that day and used those to tie them together. Margaret thought that she might not sink because of her crinoline.

According to Inkpen:

We then threw ourselves into the canal, she having put her arms round my neck. We turned over in the water two or three times, and the string or lace broke, and we separated, and she seemed to be soon drowned. I got out on the opposite side of the canal and instantly got in again, and tried to get her out, but could not find her. I then swam across the canal and got out and went home [Inkpen lived with his widowed mother]. *Before we got into the canal I was very bad and she was obliged to hold me up.*

On his way home, Inkpen met one John Rossiter, who was walking with a woman, in a lane near to the canal. Rossiter later recalled how Inkpen was very wet, as if he had been overboard and now he was running.

Inkpen did not have long to spend in his lodgings in Amelia Terrace before he received a visitor. It was Inspector Stephen Ellis of the local police. He said that he had received information from some of Inkpen's friends which necessitated the call. Ellis was told that Inkpen was upstairs in bed and so had a short wait before Inkpen arrived. Ellis and Inkpen took a short walk outside. A few of the latter's friends were nearby.

Ellis asked Inkpen, 'I suppose you can point out the spot where it occurred?' Inkpen replied, 'I can tell you all about it' and indeed he proceeded to tell Ellis the events of his day. Afterwards, as Ellis noticed that Inkpen was shivering, he asked him if he was feeling any better now. Inkpen said, 'Yes, and if I had been like this some time ago, I should not have had this charge against me.' He showed Ellis where they had attempted to jointly end their lives. The corpse was soon located there and dragged out. Inkpen asked to see her and wondered if she was disfigured. When he was permitted to see her, he exclaimed, 'She is so changed.'

Margaret Edmunds was buried at Brockley Cemetery that night, as per the law regarding suicides. Some, however, thought that she was the victim of murder, rather than one who had committed suicide, and so protested at this midnight interment. At the inquest on 12 November, Inkpen was indicted for the murder of Margaret and also as an accessory to her self-murder. Suicide, it should be noted, was at this time a criminal offence, and remained so into the twentieth century.

The trial took place at the Old Bailey on 30 November. Inkpen pleaded 'not guilty'. One of the prime questions which arose from the

Surrey Canal and the London–Greenwich Railway, 1841. London Borough of Lewisham

trial was why the events had occurred. Inkpen had certainly been drinking steadily throughout the day, and had had very little to eat. Mr Hay, the landlord of the Lord Duncan, said Inkpen was a regular customer and 'a very sober young man'. He recalled that he came to the pub at about half past seven and had drank porter. He said that he and Margaret left together and seemed to be perfectly good friends. Other witnesses described Inkpen as 'a very humane, sober, and well disposed young man'.

However, he had been drinking throughout the day. PC Turner spoke of how Inkpen had been in the Ship and Bell pub in East Greenwich on the fatal day. After the race, Inkpen had been to the pub with friends and had had brandy and beer and had only eaten a little portion of a biscuit. He had also purchased a pair of bootlaces from an itinerant vendor. These laces were the same as were later found in the canal.

On the other hand, Margaret was not described as being suicidal. Mary Ann Collins, her sister, said that she had last seen her on 10 November and described her as being 'in good spirits, as in fact, she always was'. She confirmed her friendship with Inkpen. Mrs Susannah Russell, wife of a tax inspector, and Margaret's employer, said likewise that her late servant was 'always a girl of very good spirits'. She recalled that she went out at seven o'clock in the evening for her supper beer and, at that time, 'her spirits were as usual, and she did not evince any singularity of conduct or demeanour'.

Joseph Henderson, a surgeon of Deptford High Street who examined the corpse, declared that death was due to suffocation caused by drowning. He could find no marks of violence, except a few bruises to the arm, body and head. All these would have been caused by her body falling against a hard substance, such as the side of the canal.

Mr Sleigh summed up the case for the defence. He argued that Inkpen bore no malice towards the deceased and therefore did not wilfully murder her. He also said that Inkpen was in a confused state because of his drinking and so did not really understand what was going on. He was probably acting under Margaret's direction as she had had to place her arms around his neck.

Justice Byles remarked that the case 'was most painful to all parties'. But he had to explain to the jury what the law was in these cases. Where two people agree to commit suicide and only one of them dies, the survivor is deemed guilty of murder. In this case, therefore, Inkpen was clearly guilty. The foreman of the jury asked if, as they believed, Inkpen's version of events was true, would the offence he was charged with still be murder. Byles gave a positive answer.

After a brief space of time, the jury returned after their discussion. They returned the verdict of guilty but added a recommendation for mercy. When asked they told the judge that they believed Inkpen's story and that there was no malice on his part. Inkpen was then asked if he had anything to say, but he had not. Byles donned his black cap and, in a state of great emotion, told the court that he agreed with the jury's verdict and their opinion of Inkpen's motives. He said he would make sure that the plea for mercy was forwarded to the proper authorities. However, he was then obliged to pass the death sentence.

Inkpen was taken to Maidstone Prison, accompanied by two warders from Newgate. En route, he 'frequently expressed the deepest sorrow for the melancholy occurrence'. He said that he was in such a state after the incident that he did not know what had occurred or that his companion was dead. Petitions were sent to the Home Secretary on his behalf. These were listened to and he was reprieved in the following year and gaoled for a token twelve months. By the 1870s he had returned to live in Deptford, married and had, by 1881, at least three children.

CHAPTER 12

Death in Deptford
1868

Whenever I reach patsy, I will give him three inches of this ...

Superintendent Frederick Williamson was writing a report on 28 June 1870 about a murder which had occurred two years before. It had been a regrettable affair, not only because there had been a violent death, but because the murderer had absconded and had not been brought to book. From the police's viewpoint, it was unfinished business.

What had happened was this. On 23 August 1868, Patrick Desmond, an Irish dock worker, with no known relations, and who resided in a common lodging house in New King Street, Deptford, had been stabbed. This took place at the Navy Arms, a public house in the same street in which he lodged. He was taken to Guy's Hospital, but died there two days later. An inquest was held on 4 September. The principal witness was Ellen Coates, daughter of the landlord of the Fishing Smack, a pub in the same road as the Navy Arms. She recalled that Desmond and three other men were drinking together on the afternoon of the fatal day. Desmond fell asleep. One of his companions, George Lane, wanted Jeremiah Toomey, a labourer of Walford who resided in the same lodging house as Desmond, to buy the next round. Toomey, however, claimed that he had been robbed. Ellen went to find her father. Desmond was accused of having taken four shillings and seven pence from Toomey.

Desmond protested his innocence, saying, 'I did not have it, and am willing you search me.' Toomey replied, 'Let us see whether you have anything or not.' The two men went through the passage and Desmond was searched, but to no avail.

Ellen Coates then went to the Navy Arms. At 8.30 Toomey came into the pub. He told a man called John Woods that he had been robbed and he knew who the thief was. Desmond was also present. Toomey whispered something into his ear and took hold of him with both hands in order to lead him outside. They had been gone for a few minutes when Desmond returned, staggering and obviously in a bad

Deptford High Street and New King Street (right), 1841. London Borough of Lewisham

way. He complained of being in great pain and was bleeding heavily from the chest. He muttered, 'Yes, Jerry did it.'

Sarah Duggins, a young woman who lodged in the same house as Toomey, also gave evidence against him. She recalled that, on the evening of the murder, Toomey was sharpening a knife. She also remembered that he said to her, 'Whenever I meet patsy, I will give him three inches of this.' Patsy was the nickname given to Desmond.

There were two other men present and they urged Toomey not to be violent, but he did not answer them, and shortly afterwards left the house. Later that evening one of the men returned and told Sarah that he believed that Toomey had done something to Desmond as the latter was lying bleeding on the floor of a pub.

John Woods, deputy landlord of the lodging house, said that he and Desmond had been to the pub with William Hall, and he recalled how Toomey had taken Desmond outside, as related by Ellen. Hall said that Desmond had told him that he had indeed taken money from Toomey, an action for which Hall reproved him. He also saw the two men confront each other outside the pub and said that Toomey struck the other and then thrust something into his pocket. Not realizing then that Toomey had stabbed Desmond, Hall went home.

Mr Colley of Guy's gave the medical evidence. He said that Desmond had arrived at 10.25 pm and was suffering from a wound on the left side of the body, which was about an inch deep. Death had resulted from an inflammation caused by the intestine being penetrated.

The verdict was that Toomey was responsible. The motive for the killing was that Desmond had stolen from Toomey and the latter wanted to teach him a lesson. The difficulty was that Toomey was nowhere to be found.

Notices were posted on 28 August 1868 in order to try and gain information about his whereabouts. They gave a detailed description of Toomey:

> *Age thirty; height five feet six or seven inches, complexion fair, hair light (tuft on the chin) pale face, no whiskers, thick set, high cheek bones, turn up nose, downcast look, swaggering gait, has a peculiar mode of raising the right arm below the elbow when walking; dress white duck jacket and trousers, dark vest, black or blue worsted Glengarry cap, peak of same, bound with silk, black and white check band, militia boots. A native of Cork, Ireland, is a dock labourer, and it is believed he will apply for work at large contractors, iron works, builders, etc.*

Any information was to be given to Scotland Yard. Yet this produced nothing positive. As Williamson wrote in his report two years later, 'Up to the present time, no clue was obtained as to his whereabouts.'

Yet on that very morning, Police Sergeant Watson claimed to have found Toomey at Harlesden Street, Openshaw, near Manchester, only he went by the name of Stephen Hall. He was employed as a forgeman at Ashbury's carriage works. Watson wished to arrest him, but needed someone to come up from London in order to confirm identification. The police lead had come from the fact that Toomey corresponded with his mother in London and a letter fell into the hands of the police. Williamson was only too happy for Inspector Chester to take the train to Manchester with the hope of arresting their man.

Here, at last, seemed a ray of hope. At first, everything went smoothly. Inspector Rowbotham of the Lancashire Constabulary made enquiries and the suspect was located at Harlesden Street. When the police called, he was in bed. He claimed to be one John Williams from South Wales. When questioned he admitted his real name was Jeremiah Toomey, but denied the charge of murder. Rowbotham was unconvinced, 'These circumstances appearing so suspicious, I took him to the West Gorton Police Station, where he was detained' until he could be taken by train to London.

Toomey, although protesting his innocence, did not object strongly to being taken to London. His mother lived in Poplar, he said, and so he was happy to have a visit to see her, and at no expense to himself.

King Street, later Watergate Street, c.1920. London Borough of Lewisham

Once in London, nothing went well for the police. Ellen Coates, a principal witness to the murder, identified him, but said he 'was very much alike to the man wanted, but could not speak positive to his being the one'. Worse was to come. Three other witnesses (unnamed, but presumably Sarah, Woods and Hall) all said that the prisoner was not the man in question. The police had no alternative than to release him.

Toomey was given seven shillings so as to reimburse him for his time and loss of earnings, as well as receiving a free ticket back to Manchester. Was he guilty of murder? Had the passage of time rendered the witnesses unsure as to his identity? Why was he living under a false name in Lancashire? And if he was innocent, who killed Patrick Desmond? The most probable solution was that Toomey was guilty, but could not be tried because he could not be positively identified.

CHAPTER 13

Was Montague John Druitt Jack the Ripper?
1888

I have little doubt but that his own family believed him to have been the murderer ...

Jack the Ripper is one of Britain's most infamous murderers – partly because of the horrific nature of his murders and partly because he was never caught. There are very many books on the topic and their scope is potentially endless because this unsolved mystery continues to fascinate and cause speculation, and, given present knowledge, is unsolvable. But what was the connection between him and Montague John Druitt, an apparently respectable young Blackheath schoolmaster?

It is worth briefly surveying the facts of the Ripper murders. In the poverty-stricken Whitechapel and Spitalfields districts of London's East End, prostitution was rife. In the autumn of 1888, five poor women (mostly middle-aged) were murdered in the early hours of the morning (probably) by the same assailant. These were Mary Ann Nichols (31 August), Annie Chapman (8 September), Catherine Eddowes and Elizabeth Stride (both on 30 September) and finally Mary Jane Kelly (9 November). All had had their throats cut by a sharp knife and four were terribly mutilated (Mary Kelly being the worst of all), having had some of their internal organs removed. They may have been strangled first. It is possible that the same frenzied killer began his murders earlier, with Martha Tabram, and continuing in 1889 and 1891 (Alice McKenzie and Frances Coles). It seems probable that the killer was driven by sexual or sadistic impulses rather than any rational motive. Despite an intensive campaign on the part of the police, no one was ever charged with the murders. The Police Commissioner, Sir Charles Warren, faced great press criticism and resigned his post.

But who killed these unfortunate women? Numerous theories have been expounded. The difficulty is that so little is known about the killer. There were a number of witness statements about a man seen with some of the women shortly before their deaths. These naturally differ. For example, witnesses variously claimed he was middle-aged, or in his twenties, some said he wore a bowler hat, others a peaked hat, some said he was clean shaven, others that he was moustached. It was also thought that the killer had some anatomical knowledge and that he was probably right-handed. He was probably a young man, in good physical health, a bachelor and in regular employment as the killings occurred on weekends.

There have been numerous theories as to his identity. Some have been farcical – such as the suggestion that Queen Victoria's grandson, Prince Albert Victor, was responsible (for all the murders he had cast-iron alibis). Others are less so. These include Aaron Kosminski, an insane Polish Jew who was incarcerated in an asylum shortly after the murders ceased, George Chapman (a poisoner) and many others.

Two authors, Daniel Farson and Tom Cullen, were the first to select Druitt as the killer; though many others disagree and put forward other candidates or none. Others have agreed with the Druitt thesis and there are numerous websites which attest to this. Shortly after Farson's book was published, there came *The Return of Moriarty* by John Gardner, in which Druitt is identified as the killer. They suggest Druitt's motive was to draw attention to East End poverty. Before we discuss their evidence, we need first to find out a little more about Druitt.

There are a number of indisputable facts. Druitt was born in 1857 in Wimborne, Dorset, and was from a comfortable social background. His father was a doctor. He attended Winchester College in 1870–76 and then New College, Oxford, graduating in 1880 with a third in Classics. Although not academically brilliant, he was a popular young man, taking part in theatrical productions and in the debating society (favouring liberal causes), as well as being a gifted sportsman. From at least the spring of 1881, he was assistant schoolmaster in Blackheath, at a small, but well esteemed, private boarding school for boys at Eliot Place, whose proprietor was George Valentine. In 1881, there were fifteen boys, aged between 14 and 17, boarding there. His annual salary was generous – £200 per annum, minus money for board and lodging – Druitt living at the school itself. Druitt was also an accomplished cricketer and became treasurer of the Morden Cricket Club, Blackheath, and was elected to the MCC in 1884. He was also a barrister at the Inner Temple from 1885 and was registered at King's Bench Walk. His legal work took him to the Western Circuit as special pleader. He was clearly able to combine two professions, neither of which can be regarded as being full-time.

Eliot Place, Blackheath, c.1905. London Borough of Lewisham

However, Druitt's family background was, in some ways, an unfortunate one. His father died of a heart attack in 1885 and his mother, Anne, developed delusions and was diagnosed as suffering from depression. In 1888, she was sent to the Brook Asylum in Clapton and was to die in another asylum in Chiswick in 1890. Others in the family had become insane and committed suicide. In 1888 Druitt probably developed an unknown mental disease, too, though there is no medical evidence for this. Druitt visited his eldest brother, William, a solicitor and a fellow bachelor, in Bournemouth in late October. About a month later, he was dismissed from his teaching post, for reasons which are not recorded.

A report of the inquest declared that he 'had got into serious trouble at the school'. He had been employed at the school for about eight years and was probably quite close to Valentine. It has been suggested that he was molesting the boys under his care – he would be in charge of the boys at night time when Valentine was elsewhere. Predatory homosexuals often found a niche teaching in boys' schools in order to indulge their perverted tastes. Any school known to have employed such a fellow could expect to fall in repute if not collapse altogether. However this is mere speculation, for which there is no evidence. What is more likely is that he lost his job because there were signs of his mental health deteriorating, which, as we shall see, he clearly thought it was. Mental illness was not understood at this time, being often seen as a disease, and reactions to sufferers were unsympathetic.

From photo lent by the Rev. J. T. Bramston.

WINCHESTER XI., 1876.

J. A. Fort.		A. H. Rooper.	F. S. Baines.	W. H. B. Bird.
W. R. Sheldon.	S. J. Wilson.	W. A. Thornton.	J. Eyre.	A. W Moon.
		R. B. A. Prichard.		M. J. Druitt.

Montague John Druitt and his fellows at Winchester College, 1876. Winchester College

In any case, for Druitt, this was a disaster, as he not only lost his job, but his home and his social life: a catastrophe, and on top of his mother's insanity too.

Druitt was alive on Saturday 1 December, but on 11 December it was stated that he had not been seen at his chambers for over a week. He had suffered too many mental blows in the previous few months and decided to end his life by committing suicide. The exact date of death is unknown, but 1 December seems probable as that is the date of the railway ticket to Hammersmith which was found on his body, though one account states he was last seen alive on Monday 3 December. It would appear he took the train from Charing Cross to Hammersmith, weighed his pockets down with four large stones in each and then threw himself off Hammersmith Bridge (a not un-common location for suicides then and now) and into the Thames. The tide carried him westwards towards Chiswick, where his body became stuck in the mud by Thorneycroft's Works. Henry Winslade, a waterman, found Druitt's decomposed corpse there on 31 Decem-ber. It had been there for a few weeks. A tragic end to a promising life.

The Acton Gazette gave an account of the inquest of 2 January. Cheques made payable to him for £50 and £16 were found on his body; perhaps for arrears of salary and a pay off in lieu of notice of dismissal. William Druitt related that his brother had not been seen at his chambers at King's Walk since early December, so he went up to Blackheath and searched his brother's rooms there. He had found a note addressed to him, which read 'Since Friday [30 November?] I felt I was going to be like mother, and the best thing for me was to die.' Valentine had also received a letter from Druitt, presumably with a similar thrust. Druitt had never threatened to take his life before. A verdict of suicide whilst in a state of unsound mind was returned. For what it is worth, the local paper gave a laudatory notice of Druitt, on his death:

> *The deceased was well known and much respected in the neighbour-hood. He was a barrister of bright talent, he had a promising future before him and his untimely end is deeply deplored.*

Druitt was buried in Wimborne Cemetery on the day after the inquest. In 1891 his personal estate of £2,600 2s was transmitted to William; an indication, at least, that his legal career had been financially rewarding. An examination of the administration of his effects indicates nothing of note. As a comparison, when Inspector Frederick Abberline, one of the detectives investigating the Ripper murders, died in 1929, he left £317.

There seems nothing in this brief account of the life and death of Druitt which would indicate that he was a mass murderer, or in any way violent or misogynistic. However, researchers have found evidence to suggest that at least one senior policeman had had his suspicions about him.

The relevant evidence is found in two versions of what is known as the MacNaghten Memorandum; confidential notes only made available in recent decades. Sir Melville MacNaghten was an Assistant Chief Constable at Scotland Yard, albeit after the Ripper murders had taken place. In one of these, written in 1894 to exonerate one Thomas Cutbush (whose uncle was a senior policeman), accused in the press of the murders, he discusses three men who he thought might have been more likely to have been guilty.

MacNaghten wrote thus:

> *the murderer's brain gave way altogether after his awful glut in Miller's Court* [the murder of Mary Jane Kelly] *and that he immediately committed suicide, or as a possible alternative, was found to be so hopelessly mad by his relations, that he was by them confined in some asylum ... A Mr. M.J. Druitt, said to be a doctor & of good family,*

Gravestone of Montague John Druitt, Wimborne Cemetery, 2006. Somerset and Devon Family History Society

who disappeared at the time of the Miller's Court murder, & whose body (which was said to have been upward of a month in the water) was found in the Thames on 31st. Decr, or about 7 weeks after that murder. He was sexually insane and from private inf. I have little doubt but that his own family believed him to have been the murderer.

He also wrote, in another version of the Memorandum which has now disappeared:

I enumerate the cases of three men against whom the police held very reasonable suspicion. Personally, after much careful & deliberate consideration, I am inclined to exonerate the last two, but I have always held strong opinions regarding no. 1 [Druitt], and the more I think the matter over, the stronger do these opinions become. The truth, however, will never be known, and did indeed, at one time lie at the bottom of the Thames, if my conjections be correct.

In his published memoirs, written two decades later, MacNaghten wrote of the unnamed killer, 'his brain gave way altogether and he committed suicide, otherwise the murders would not have ceased' and 'the individual who held London in terror resided with his own people; that he absented himself from home at certain times, that he committed suicide on or about the 10th of November 1888'.

Major Arthur Griffiths, a prison inspector, also wrote his memoirs and made a similar observation, but did not name the killer,

He was a doctor in the prime of life, was believed to be insane . . . and he disappeared immediately after the last murder, that in Miller's Court on the 9th of November 1888. On the last day of that year, seven weeks later his body was found floating in the Thames and was said to have been in the water a month.

There was allegedly a booklet, *The East End Murderer – I knew him*, written by Druitt's cousin, Lionel, in Australia about Druitt being the killer. However, on investigation, the book proved to be unavailable, assuming it ever existed. It is certainly not located in the Australian National Library.

Apparently one of the pupils at his old school was aware of these suspicions in the 1890s, but we do not know who and why. It was also noted that his carved initials at the school were made by a sharp knife. A West Country MP also reported the rumour that the Ripper was a doctor who drowned himself.

Around these memoirs and comments, those who believe Druitt was the Ripper assemble an array of apparently impressive circumstantial evidence. It is argued that Druitt had always lived in all-male environments – at school, at college and at work – and so he may have developed strange attitudes to women, which led him to being a serial murderer. Although he could not have caught a train back to Blackheath after the murders (they did not run in the early hours of the morning), he could have used his legal chambers in King's Bench Walk as a base for his murders. Descriptions of the killer claim he had a moustache, was aged in his thirties and appeared to be respectable: 'shabbily genteel'. This would fit Druitt. As a cricketer, he would have been fairly strong and possessed a degree of manual dexterity – useful for cutting throats. Finally he was a doctor's son, so would have had access to books about anatomy.

Steve White, who had worked as a policeman during the murders, recalled seeing a well-dressed, well-spoken man in the vicinity of Elizabeth Stride's corpse. Could this have been Druitt? However, White, who did not name his suspect, went on to say 'altogether the man was foreign in appearance', which seems to rule Druitt out. One authority on the Ripper suggests that White's remarks refer to the

King's Bench Walk, 2006. The author

murder of Alice McKenzie in 1889 – by which time Druitt was already dead.

Druitt might have known the East End well because his cousin, Dr Lionel Druitt, once worked in his medical capacity in the Minories in the City of London in 1879, before emigrating to Australia. Druitt may have visited his cousin. Druitt may have been involved or interested in work among the poor and the deprivation there and this may have unhinged his already weak mind. These two hypotheses explain Druitt's connection with the East End. Furthermore, Druitt has no alibi for any of the murders. Finally, the five definite Ripper killings stopped after his death by suicide – serial killers rarely stop unless they are arrested or die.

An ingenious alternative theory was propounded by Stephen Knight, who stated that Druitt, though not the murderer, was the scapegoat for a murderous conspiracy carried out by the Freemasons. Knight made a number of tenuous connections between Druitt and the conspirators and alleges that they killed him in early December, intending him to take the blame for the murders. However, Knight produces no evidence to suggest that Druitt was murdered. Another theory suggests that Druitt and one James Stephens, Prince Albert Victor's former tutor, collaborated in the murders. This is another complex conspiracy theory, based on surmise and hypotheses.

All this is very hypothetical. The contemporary evidence is certainly ambiguous. It is also inaccurate. The police seem to have had very little information about Druitt or evidence against him. MacNaghten and Griffiths state that Druitt was a doctor and that he disappeared immediately after the killing of Mary Kelly. Both these facts are incorrect. Nor did he commit suicide directly after the murder just cited. Nor did Druitt reside with his family as MacNaghten thought. There was no further investigation into Druitt, as there would have been if he really had been suspected. Nor did the heavy (and expensive) police presence in the East End cease after Druitt's death. The case was not officially closed until 1892. Needless to say, there is no file about Druitt in the archives of the Metropolitan Police. MacNaghten is very vague about Druitt and seems uncertain himself about the man's guilt. Nowhere is there a shred of evidence against him. Why MacNaghten suspected him is unknown. It may have been because of his suicide coinciding with the end of the five definite killings (suicide was a criminal offence and so Druitt's case would have been known to the police). Needless to say, there is no indication as to what this 'private inf.' he mentioned consisted of, assuming there was any. Where would he have got it from? Neither Druitt's family nor his colleagues would have been likely to have told him anything incriminating, especially since he was dead. It is also worth noting MacNaghten's comment: 'No one ever saw the Whitechapel Murderer, many homicidal maniacs were suspected, but no shadow of proof could be thrown on anyone.' The hypotheses built on the Memorandum thus fall like a pack of cards.

Not all contemporary policemen agreed with MacNaghten. Abberline discounted the possibility of Druitt being guilty. He said,

> *But what does it amount to? Simply this. Soon after the last murder in Whitechapel the body of a young doctor was found in the Thames, but there is nothing beyond the fact that he was found to incriminate him ... there is much more reason to think the man emigrated ... the fact that several months after December, 1888, when the student's body was found, the detectives were told still to hold themselves in readiness for further investigations seems to point to the conclusion that Scotland Yard did not in any way consider the evidence as 'final'.*

Abberline also said in 1903, when asked about Druitt, 'You can state most emphatically that Scotland Yard is really no wiser on the subject than it was fifteen years ago. It is simple nonsense to talk of the police having proof that the man is dead.' Again, note the lack of real knowledge about Druitt; in calling him a doctor Abberline repeats MacNaghten's error. Other police chiefs suspected Aaron Kosminski.

As to the circumstantial 'evidence', much is merely surmise and hypothesis. Many men lived in all-male environments, and whatever attitudes they may have had about women, they did not subsequently turn to serial killing. As to the descriptions of the killer, Druitt was slender – but the killer is said to been either medium or heavily built. Nor was he foreign-looking as some witnesses stated. It is also worth noting that it seems unlikely that a well-heeled young man would haunt the denizens of the poor in the dead of night where he risked being robbed and assaulted. It has also been pointed out that the killer left the scene of the second murder in a north-easterly direction, when, if he was returning to his chambers, he would have walked westwards. On this topic, it should also be realized that the chambers at King's Walk were nothing but a business address (shared by a number of other barristers); certainly they did not resemble a bachelor pad to which Druitt could retire to at night. The 1901 census, for instance, notes that no one was resident here. Had Druitt killed women in the East End as claimed he would have had to loiter there unseen until the first train left in the morning (unless he had lodgings there, but this put him into someone else's hands), a very unlikely hypothesis. If, as seems likely, Druitt was suffering from melancholia (i.e. depression) as his mother was, he would hardly be likely to turn to murder – paranoid schizophrenics might, but not depressives. If he was homosexual, he would not be killing women but men.

On the morning of 9 September, the murder took place at about 5.30 am Druitt is known to have been playing cricket at Blackheath six hours later. Could a man who would have had to have been stalking the streets all night really have played cricket on the same morning? On another occasion, he was playing cricket in Dorset on the morning of another murder. No one noticed any mental deterioration in him until late November 1888 – he continued his legal work and spoke at cricket meetings. It is also worth noting that very few people's movements of over a century ago are known, so the fact that he does not have an alibi is hardly a strong point against him. In any case, most people are asleep in bed in the early hours and as he was a bachelor he would hardly have anyone to vouch for him. Finally, if the Ripper murders are not restricted to the five women who were inarguably his victims, and they did indeed carry on until 1891, Druitt cannot have been responsible for he was already dead by then.

Druitt does not fit the psychological profile of serial killers, nor does he resemble any of the known ones. These men are usually loners, social misfits and inadequates who kill to prove that they are somebodies. They also kill in neighbourhoods which they know well and so can move freely about. They rarely commit suicide. Druitt appears to have been socially successful and certainly does not fit such a profile. The real killer was probably a very nondescript man of this kind who lived in the East End and was suspected by no one. His identity may never be known. One theory is that Edward Buchan, a marine store dealer of Mile End, who also drowned himself at the end of the year, is a more likely candidate than Druitt.

It is impossible to prove that Druitt was innocent. But it is up to the 'prosecution' to find him guilty or cease their accusations. And this they cannot do. The evidence against him is extremely thin as to be almost non-existent and is largely conjectural. It seems more likely that he was developing a form of insanity – though he was able to continue being a lawyer and schoolmaster during the period of the murders, so its initial effect until the last moment was minimal. MacNaghten's comment about family sources claiming he was responsible is vague and unsubstantiated. If the police really thought he was guilty, there is the question as to why they did not investigate his background and why there is not any extant file about him. There is no evidence as to why he should kill the unfortunate women. Almost any man in London could have killed them, after all. What is most likely is that Druitt believed he was becoming insane and, shortly after losing his job, committed suicide. The fact that this was a few weeks after the murder of Mary Kelly is almost certainly coincidence. He is more to be pitied for his illness and his tragic end than to be blamed for mass murder. Unfortunately he has been much maligned by those for whom he is more interesting as a mass murderer than the frail human being he ultimately became.

The Ripper's fame certainly spread locally. As will be noted in the following chapter, a Deptford serial killer was referred to as Jack the Ripper in 1889. In the same year, James Connell, an Irish draper living in New Cross Road, was interviewed by the police because a woman he had been walking with was alarmed by his talking about the Ripper and asylums. He was found to be innocent. Another local reference was that, on 21 June 1891, Moses Arnold, a basket maker and seller, was seen behaving oddly at Grove Park Railway Station. Apparently he tried to cut his own throat with a sharp piece of flint. A railway official and a policeman managed to restrain him and put him into custody. As he was trying to commit suicide, Arnold shouted that he was 'Jack the Ripper'. And a murder on Blackheath in 1931 (Chapter 22) was described as being 'a Ripper murder'. The unidentified killer's legacy was very much apparent both locally and nationally.

CHAPTER 14

The Deptford Poisonings
1888–89

I assure you that the most winning woman I ever knew was hanged for poisoning three little children for their insurance money.

(Sherlock Holmes, in *The Sign of Four*, 1890)

Readers of detective fiction may be aware of a detective novel by Julian Symons, *The Blackheath Poisonings*. It has fine period detail, and tells of an upper middle-class family, some of whose members are killed by poison. It can be highly recommended but is, of course, fiction. Poisoning was, in fact, rare, as a means of murder in real life, as can be seen in this book. There is only one poisoning case that was ever brought to light in the district covered by this book, and that happened at Deptford and to people somewhat lower the down the social scale. It also concerns one of the most prolific murderesses in British history.

Death was common in the nineteenth century, as it had been in earlier centuries. Poor living conditions, the lack of ready medicines and bad diet all contributed, especially in the overcrowded housing which was prevalent in most of Deptford. If people died, unless it was by violent means, it was hardly something to be shocked at, especially if they were old or young.

There were a number of deaths in Deptford in 1888 and 1889 which were apparently due to natural causes. Mrs Elizabeth Frost, aged forty-seven, lodged in a room in Old King Street. She earned money by washing and mending clothes. Unfortunately, in early February 1888, she began to be unwell.

On 3 February, Mrs Emma Dalamain of Czar Street was told by her sister about their mother being ill. Visiting her mother, Mrs Dalamain found her thus:

She said she felt very bad, and was in dreadful pain in her stomach. Her face was very much swollen. She was dreadfully thirsty and sick, and

had diarrhoea and could not keep anything down. She said she felt very
bad before this.

Apparently she had been doing some washing at Mrs Amelia Winters's house in Church Street, and felt ill. She was given brandy. She had also been sick.

Mrs Elizabeth Frost had not been neglected. Mrs Winters and Thomas Frost, Mrs Elizabeth Frost's son, had been to see her regularly, usually once a day, and they had brought her food, including beef tea, whisky, brandy and oranges. But the beef tea made the patient sick and the brandy burnt her mouth. Dr Macnaughton was called in. Mrs Winters said Mrs Frost was suffering from bronchitis, according to the doctor. Mrs Dalamain wanted a second opinion and was to call in Dr Hingston, the parish doctor, on 6 February. Hingston suggested removal to an infirmary, but Macnaughton disagreed and became very angry.

Death was on 7 February. Macnaughton wrote the death certificate. He thought she had been suffering from chronic alcoholism, as well as bronchitis and a weak heart, based on her symptoms. He said,

In my opinion she had been a drunken woman and stomatitis would
have been the result of drinking. I based my opinions from her general
symptoms and the bloated appearance of her face.

He disagreed with the suggestion that he had opposed the sending for another medical man.

Mrs Elizabeth Frost's life had been insured and Thomas Frost and Emma Dalamain were the beneficiaries. Mrs Elizabeth Jane Frost (hereafter Mrs Frost), Mrs Frost's daughter-in-law and Mrs Winters's eldest daughter, and Mrs Winters, had paid the premiums for these policies. It did not seem at all remarkable to anyone that a poor, middle-aged woman who was fond of alcohol should die.

The second death aroused little curiosity, either. William Sutton, a widower, had been a resident of the Greenwich Workhouse for some years, residing in the ward for the infirm, though his health was good for an old man (variously described as aged seventy-four or seventy-nine) and he had had no medical treatment since May 1888. On the morning of 4 December 1888 he left the workhouse for a day's outing and never returned. On the following day, William Henry Jordan, the master of the workhouse, received a letter from an address in Church Street, Deptford, to tell him that Sutton was ill and was being looked after. Jordan could not recall who the writer was, and had lost the letter. It said Sutton was unlikely to return, so Jordan crossed his name off his books. The workhouse clothes were soon returned.

Mrs Mary Ann Winters was Sutton's daughter and had married a labourer of Deptford. They lived in Berthon Street. She often visited

Lewisham Workhouse, c.1905. London Borough of Lewisham

her partly senile, partly blind father in the workhouse. He was by now a very ill man. Sutton went to stay with Mrs Amelia Winters, the mother-in-law of Mrs Mary Winters. Unfortunately for Sutton, moving out of the workhouse resulted in a rapid deterioration of his health. On the following days he was sick and suffered much from vomiting. Dr Macnaughton was called and he concluded that the change in his diet was probably the cause of the patient's illness, as Sutton had enjoyed a hearty meal after leaving the workhouse, but was optimistic that he should shortly recover and would then be able to return to the workhouse. None of the medicines he gave – cerium, opium, soda and gentian and a drachma of chlorodyne – contained anything which would injure him. Sutton was given broth by Mrs Winters senior. On 8 December, Sutton seemed better, but later he suffered a fit and died. On the death certificate, the cause of death was recorded as senile decay.

Mrs Winters senior had taken out an insurance policy with the Prudential on Sutton's death in August 1886. She had paid six pence a week, but had later increased the payments by an extra four pence a week in the following year. Apparently the policy was to ensure that there was enough money to bury him properly: nothing curious in that.

Children, often the most vulnerable age group, continued to die young in this era and into the early twentieth century. Sydney and

Mary Ann, his fourteen-year-old sister, were the children of James Samuel Bolton, of Creek Street, Deptford, an employee of Hill's chemical works. Being separated from his wife, he decided to have the children board with his aunt. Therefore, in 1887, the two were boarding with Mr and Mrs Winters. She was paid ten shillings a week towards the children's living expenses. The arrangement seemed to be working well. Bolton saw his children twice or thrice a week and later declared that Sydney was in good health.

However, Sydney developed diarrhoea in January 1889 and Bolton was too busy to see him for another fortnight. At first he did not think his son's illness was serious, but when he finally visited he thought Sydney looked very ill and thin. Sydney complained of a pain in the stomach. Dr Macnaughton once more had been in attendance and said the lad had been very sick. Matters worsened. Mrs Winters summoned Bolton and he found his son to be in a very bad way. He had had two fits and was perpetually thirsty. His concerned father now visited him every night. Sydney's brother, James, also visited him and was told about pains in the back and stomach. He was looked after by Mrs Winters and her daughter, Mrs Frost, who lived next door. Unfortunately, Sydney's condition worsened and on 11 February he died. The death certificate was issued on the following day,

Church Street, Deptford, 1890s. London Borough of Lewisham

stating that he had died because of diarrhoea and convulsions: perfectly normal, however tragic an event.

Before the funeral took place, the grieving father spoke to Mrs Winters. He reminded her that when she took his children into care, she promised to pay a penny a week insurance to the Prudential Office on their behalf, and a halfpenny for any doctor's fees, out of the ten shillings he gave her for their keep. Mrs Winters told him that she had not kept up with the payments and so the policy had expired. Bolton made enquiries at the insurance company and they told him that Mrs Winters had been paid £10 by them. The £10 had been paid back and later Mrs Winters had received £3 and £7 was given to Bolton, half of which he paid towards the funeral expenses.

In the following month, Bolton's suspicions were aroused when he discovered that Mrs Winters had received £20 for Sydney's death from the Liverpool Victoria Insurance Company. He did not tell Mrs Winters of his findings, but instead informed the police. He recalled that his daughter had been ill prior to Sydney's illness, and that he had made his final payment to Mrs Winters on the day before his son died. The police agreed that the circumstances seemed to merit investigation and an order was made by none other than the Secretary of State himself, in early April, that the corpse be exhumed.

On 22 April, at the Breakspear Arms in Brockley, an inquest was held to ascertain the cause of Sydney's death. The body had been removed from its grave in Brockley Cemetery. Some of the organs were removed and sent to Guy's Hospital for analysis.

At the inquest, the jury viewed the corpse and its identity was confirmed. The inquest was then adjourned to await the results of the medical examination at the hospital. It was a serious case. It was possible that poison might have been the cause of death.

The inquest was resumed on 30 May. Investigations had uncovered the fact that Mrs Winters (who was too unwell to attend) had insured the lives of another twenty-two local people and, of these, a total of five had died and she had benefited from the death benefits paid out by insurance companies. Dr Thomas Stevenson (1838–1908), the most eminent forensic toxicologist of his day, had analysed the organs and made the startling discovery that there were traces of arsenic therein. Walter Martin, chief clerk in the claims department of the Prudential Assurance office, stated that the firm had a dozen policies in the name of Mrs Winters of Church Street, Deptford. Two were on Sydney's life, for £10 each, but only one had been paid. Had he lived two days longer, another £10 would have been paid. Mary Ann Bolton, Sydney's sister, recalled that Mrs Winters always saw to their meals. She had been sick in October 1888, after meals and after being given medicine. Her tea tasted unpleasant and she ceased drinking it,

Brockley Cemetery, c.1910. London Borough of Lewisham

which annoyed Mrs Winters. Mary Ann Edson, who had nursed Sydney for four days before his death, said that he did not eat, but often complained of being thirsty and had a peculiar fit.

It is worth considering arsenic for a moment. It was the most commonly used poison in English poisoning cases between 1750 and 1914, accounting for 45 per cent of the whole. This was because it was cheap – perhaps two pence per ounce, and easy to get hold of, though purchasers had to sign the poison book on purchase by the 1880s. It was also used to destroy domestic rodents and had other legitimate uses. Its symptoms could be mistaken for other illnesses, so had the advantage that death by poisoning might go unnoticed, making matters much safer for the poisoner. Finally, it had little taste. Yet tests which could detect arsenic were available – all that was needed was suspicion on the part of a concerned observer, whether a relative of the victim, doctor or policeman, and it was becoming more difficult for the poisoner to gain access to poison and to escape detection.

The inquest also investigated the death of William Sutton. Stephen Berry, collector for the Liverpool Victoria Legal and Friendly Society, said that Mrs Winters had insured Sutton's life with them for £8 14s on 23 July 1887. Berry had seen Sutton and Mrs Winters and assumed the two were related, but did not know if Sutton knew his life was insured. He added that it was possible to insure someone's life without them being aware of it. The premiums were regularly paid but he did not think there was anything suspicious about it nor that Sutton was a workhouse pauper. His colleague, Martin, told the court that there were two policies on Sydney's life and three on Sutton's. Between April 1884 and January 1889, his company had accepted fourteen policies on Mrs Winters's behalf.

William Coleman of the Prudential explained what had happened after Sydney died. Mrs Winters and Mrs Frost came to the office on 11 February. The latter claimed to be Sydney's mother. She said that she was Sarah Bolton and was asked to sign to confirm this, but Mrs Frost said she was illiterate. Instead she made a mark and this was witnessed by one Emma Greenway (another of Mrs Winters's daughters). Two days later, Coleman asked them if Sydney's father was alive, to which they answered he had been dead for six months. Therefore, Mrs Frost, as the child's mother, would be paid and a witness was required – this was Thomas Frost, her husband. Coleman eventually met Bolton and the payments were made as has already been described, though only after William Baker, a colleague of Coleman's, intervened and said the money would have to be returned as it was obtained by a misrepresentation. Mrs Winters said that a family quarrel was the cause of such activity and Baker did not involve the police. Coleman identified Mrs Frost in court.

Mrs Frost was then examined. She pleaded that she was wholly innocent of any wrongdoing. She claimed she did not know that her mother paid into so many insurance companies, though she did make the payments sometimes. Although she recalled making the mark mentioned above, she said that she did not know what the sum was and denied she claimed to be Sarah Bolton. She also said she had never seen any trace of arsenic. The deputy coroner said they would not find anything useful from her.

Mary Ann Bolton then gave her evidence. She explained that Mrs Winters did all the family cooking. She had been ill in the previous autumn; being sick after meals and finding the tea tasting unpleasant. There had been a 'bad pain' in her stomach on these occasions. Then she began to cry and so the examination was brought to an end.

When she felt able to resume, she told the court that Dr Macnaughton visited her, and Mrs Winters, Mrs Frost and Emma Greenway brought her meals, though her sickness continued. Her father suggested she go to hospital, but Mrs Winters was against this, persuading Mary that they were nasty places. Then she got better. The only white powder that she knew about was that which her father used to stuff birds, but she had never seen Sydney use it. As with Sutton, she did not know her life was insured.

The inquest was adjourned for a second time, but a picture of what had happened was beginning to emerge. Three days later, the inquest continued. The court at the pub in Brockley was crowded. The court was now investigating the death of Sutton, as well as that of Sydney. Mr Wood, the deputy coroner, thought it probable that Sutton's death was not due to natural causes either. The jury went to the cemetery and Sutton's body was briefly disinterred so that it might be viewed. Jordan confirmed that the corpse was that of Sutton.

Jordan and Mrs Mary Winters recounted their experiences of the previous year as regards Sutton. Macnaughton then spoke. He said he was uncertain as to precise dates as he had lost his attendance book. He had suspected that as Sutton was nearly blind he might have consumed something harmful and could not account for his symptoms. He thought the vomiting odd and told that there was not even a trace of arsenic in the medicines he had prescribed. Percy Crampton, a clerk of the Liverpool Victoria Legal Friendly Society, also gave evidence. The inquest was again adjourned.

The final day of the inquests was 9 July. By this time, another corpse had been exhumed – that of Mrs Frost, the mother-in-law of Mrs Winter's daughter, Mrs Elizabeth Frost. She had died on 7 February 1888 and had, as said, been insured by Mrs Winters. Various witnesses described her last days, and the insurance agents gave their evidence. Dr Bond told the court that Sydney and Sutton's internal organs indicated that they had been poisoned, probably by arsenic. Mrs Frost's organs were remarkably preserved and free from that decomposition that would be usual for a corpse which was over a year old, which suggested that she had been killed by the same method.

Mr Wood put some of the blame for these deaths on the insurance companies. He said:

> *To my mind the facilities given by some insurance companies to effect wholesale life insurance are direct incentives to wicked persons to destroy such lives for the sake of the insurance money ... there is nothing to prevent an adult life from being insured at the same time in several offices unknown to each other, and so that the amount insured in this way on one life may amount to a considerable sum.*

Wood also went on to censure Macnaughton's conduct. Had he not signed the death certificate of Mrs Elizabeth Frost, there would have had to have been an inquest and this would probably have saved the lives of Sydney and Sutton. Although Wood pointed the finger of suspicion, based on the evidence of the insurance policies, at Mrs Frost and Mrs Winters, he also noted that no one had seen any arsenic in their possession. He therefore asked the jury to consider the evidence and arrive at their verdict.

This they eventually did, after forty minutes of debate. Their unanimous verdict in all three cases was one of wilful murder by Mrs Winters and Mrs Frost. They followed Wood's lead in being critical of both the insurance companies' practices and Macnaughton. The witnesses at the inquest were bound over for the sum of £40 each to attend the trial at the Old Bailey on 29 July.

Mrs Frost, who was present at the inquest with her baby and her husband, was arrested by the police. She was charged with the three murders and taken away by cab to the police station. Her mother did not attend the inquest because she was too ill to do so and there was talk that she was dying. Dr Taylor, the police surgeon, certified that this was indeed the case. Mrs Frost was later charged with the attempted murder of Mary Ann Bolton.

The inquests caused a great deal of understandable concern and anger in the neighbourhood and this resulted in hostility towards Mrs Winters's family. When Mrs Frost returned from the inquest on 3 June, she found that her neighbours were waiting for her. A crowd of about 400 women threw stones and flour at her husband and her. They were unable to go home but had to take shelter under the arches of the Greenwich railway bridge. They were unable to return home for several hours, such was the anger aimed at Mrs Frost and her mother.

On 12 July Mrs Winters's condition worsened and it was feared that she might not live much longer. She was almost skeletal as she had been taking very little food. Her relatives urged her to confess to her crimes, if indeed she was guilty, partly to exonerate her daughter. William Winters, her son, visited her on the morning of the same day. He leaned over her bed and the following dialogue took place.

> *Mother, if you have done anything, pray tell me.*
> *My boy, I have ruined the family.*
> *Never mind, mother: whatever you have done, tell me. Do you know anything about old Mrs Frost and giving her anything?*
> *Yes.*
> *Who gave it to her?*
> *I gave it to her.*
> *Does Liza know anything about it?*
> *No, she knows nothing about it; nobody knew anything but myself.*
> *Where did you get the arsenic from?*
> *I did not know what arsenic was.*
> *What was it you gave her?*
> *It is what you use for the head, for the vermin – precipitate powder.*

Does Liza know anything about the death of the old man and the boy?

They are all as innocent as the babe just born.

Did you give them something?

Yes. I ask you all to forgive me. Do not say anything about this till I am dead.

Other family members, such as Emma Greenway and Annie Lewis, Mrs Winters's daughters, had similar conversations with their mother. The Revd Dr Cundy was called for to hear the confession, but he could not be found. Mrs Winters died on the following morning due to atrophy being brought on by exhaustion. There was no evidence of poisoning or foul play. She was, after all, an elderly woman.

Her burial was a difficult affair to manage because so many local people hated her (references to Jack the Ripper were made in connection with the deceased woman) and wanted to mount a demonstration. Police had to be on hand and it was announced that the burial would take place in a cemetery in Essex. However, the coffin was taken to be placed in Brockley Cemetery. A number of people did manage to gather there to try and disrupt proceedings, but the police presence deterred them and they withdrew.

Mrs Frost was charged on remand on 22 July. The confession of Mrs Winters, though not legal proof as it had been only made in the presence of family members, was important in one respect. White precipitate powder might indeed have been used to kill the victims because it produced a disagreeable taste and all victims had complained of this. Arsenic, on the other hand, is tasteless. Mercury, which appears in the precipitate powder, was found in all three bodies. It was thought possible that both substances had been used to murder the three. The charges of murder against Mrs Frost were therefore dropped because of lack of evidence.

Yet she was still charged with forgery, and witnesses testified to the fact that she had signed herself as Sarah Bolton when she and her mother went to collect the insurance money after the death of Sydney. Her defence argued that Sydney's father had not been defrauded in any way because Mrs Winters and he had shared the money received from the policy, although he did admit that the document which his client had signed was not exactly a true one, either. It was concluded that the document was a false one, and then the question became one of intent. Her defence counsel claimed that 'she had been the dupe in the hands of a wicked woman'.

The jury found her guilty, but recommended that mercy be shown. This was on the grounds that she may have been led on by her mother.

However, the jury was asked to withdraw their recommendation because, if two people conspired together, the offence was greater not lesser. Yet the sentencing was postponed because the jury had to consider three murder cases. The matter did not come to a close until the hearing on 25 October, in which Mrs Frost was sentenced to seven years imprisonment with hard labour.

The motive for these murders was clearly money. But was this due to greed or also to fear? Fear of old age, poverty and the workhouse? Mrs Winters was born in 1816 and her husband, a bricklayer, was a year older. Some might view her actions, as cold-blooded and calculatingly murderous as they were, in this sympathetic light. Yet, as noted, her neighbours had no such sympathy with her, and they were probably in similar economic circumstances.

What was the truth of the matter? It certainly seems that Mrs Winters was the criminal mastermind who had insured many lives in her neighbourhood, often choosing people who could die with no one asking any questions. These included people in her own family. They were then given arsenic and the white precipitate powder and would die of apparently natural causes. This system was helped by the fact that doctors, here Dr Macnaughton, were lax in signing death certificates and because the insurance companies were poorly managed. Mrs Winters's motive was financial, but it is hard to know the extent of the involvement of others, notably Mrs Frost, who certainly seems to have been involved along with her mother, but against whom there was little evidence and so she had to be tried on the lesser charge of forgery, for which evidence was strong. Finally, had it not been for Sydney's father, the whole conspiracy might not have come to light until more deaths have occurred much later. For Mrs Winters, in retrospect, Sydney Bolton's death had been one too many. We do not know who the other two victims were – the first apparently died in July 1886. In all there had been five murders.

In some ways, the case is not untypical of nineteenth-century poisoning cases. The poisoners were working-class and greedy; their victims were members of the extended family. They were also female – women made up about half of all poisoners, but only 13 per cent of poisoners worked in pairs. Finally, a common motive for such crimes was the financial one. At least in this case these poisonings came to an end in 1889. This series of murders, committed for the sake of insurance money, was the last of this type known to have been committed in England; it was becoming more difficult to purchase poison and insurance companies were becoming less lax.

CHAPTER 15

Murder in Deptford
1897

I am a murderer, and have come to give myself up ...

Deptford can be seen as a centre of violent crime, at least historically. One reason might be because it was heavily populated and many of these people often lived in great deprivation which could erupt into violence. The appalling murders by the insane Cavilla and the very sane killings of the old couple by the Stratton brothers will be discussed in due course, but there was a violent and multiple slaying which came first.

On the morning of Wednesday 7 June 1897, Police Sergeant Herbert Elwood was on duty at the police station at Prince Street, Deptford. Edward Callaghan, a forty-year-old local man, came into the building. He was described as being

> *a tall, powerful looking man, with dark forbidding face, his black hair cropped so close to the skull as to give one the impression he was a greyhound. A black moustache, drooping at the ends, accentuates a cruel mouth.*

Seeing him, Elwood asked him what his business was. Callaghan replied, 'Don't you know?' Elwood answered in the negative. 'My name is Edward Callaghan, and I am a murderer, and have come to give myself up, as you will run me down if I don't.'

It was hardly a usual declaration even in Deptford. Elwood was quick to point out that Callaghan should not make any statement which could be later used against him. But he did ask when and where the unspecified murder had occurred, and was met with an enigmatic reply, 'You will know soon.' Elwood noticed blood on Callaghan's right hand and asked how it came to be there. Again, he was given the enigmatic answer, 'You will soon know.'

Meanwhile, a shocking discovery was being made by one of Elwood's colleagues, PC Spuffard. He had been summoned to an address in Copperas Square, Bronze Street, Deptford, where he was shown the corpses of Mary Ann Evenden, aged forty-two, and her

Deptford Police Station, Prince Street, 1920s. London Borough of Lewisham

eldest daughter, Ann Evenden, aged eighteen. Mary was lying on a mattress in a room downstairs. Both had had their throats cut. A blood-stained pocket knife was later found under the elder woman's knee.

Callaghan, already detained on suspicion, was formally charged with murder at 9.30 am by Detective Inspector Gummer. Callaghan was remanded, and the gaol surgeon was told to make a report on the state of the prisoner's mind. Callaghan said nothing. On his person was found a bloody handkerchief and he told the police where his lethal knife was. He was sent to prison.

At the well-attended inquest held at the lecture hall of the Congregational Church in Deptford High Street, on 8 June, details of the *dramatis personae* emerged. Edward Callaghan was living with his sister's family, his sister being the late Mary Ann Evenden. Her husband was William, a bricklayer, and apart from Ann, they had two other children, William, aged nine, and Jane, aged fourteen. Evenden was clearly upset and often needed the support of a friend who accompanied him to the court. He told how his brother-in-law was formerly employed as a porter at the docks, but had been ill recently, and so was out of work. Although Callaghan had 'never said a wrong word to him [Evenden]', relations between Callaghan and his sister were sour. She had recently told him, 'We can't afford to keep you.' He replied, 'You are a wicked woman.'

Ann backed up her mother, and told him, 'Mother has quite enough trouble of her own, without your trouble.' Jane Blackmore, a neighbour, later recalled, 'I have heard frequent disturbances between him and Mrs Evenden.' Another neighbour, Mrs Stevens, had over-heard much of the quarrelling which went on, though she said that she had not meant to eavesdrop. Callaghan decided to interrupt her: 'Not because you are not paid for listening anyway. A "nose", that is what

Deptford Congregational Church, 1860s. London Borough of Lewisham

you are.' A 'nose' was then a slang expression for a police spy. His outburst confirmed the suspicions of some that he was a maniac. The coroner asked Callaghan if he wanted to question the witness and the latter said:

> *This woman is paid by the police to do nothing but watch me. She has dogged my footsteps day and night ever since I have been there. I want to let the jury and the reporters to know all about it. She's paid to do it. She had an excursion last Saturday – she was sent away.*

The widower could not let this outburst go unanswered and he said, 'Still, you'd no business to do it, Uncle Ned, you did wrong – you know it. That's straight; I'm here; you had no occasion to do it.'

Medical evidence was read out by Dr Taylor, the police surgeon. He said that the cut on Mrs Evenden's throat was three inches long and deep enough to sever everything to the root of the tongue. Her hands were wounded too, probably when she tried to prevent herself from being killed. Her daughter's spinal cord had been cut. Death would have been swift. Both murders had required great force.

The jury found it to be a case of wilful murder by Callaghan.

The magistrates' court hearing on 9 June yielded more facts. Evenden said that his brother-in-law had been staying at their house for three weeks, sleeping in the kitchen, and was usually employed at the docks as a porter. On the morning of the murder, Evenden left home for work at 6.00 am, after seeing his wife for what would be the last time. Forty-five minutes later, his son awoke. He soon heard his mother screaming downstairs. His sister, Ann, also heard the screams and she, tragically, was the first on the scene. She cried out 'Oh! My mother! Oh! My mother!' before screaming. She had good reason to.

When Charles followed her downstairs, he saw a horrific sight, as he later recalled:

> *I saw mother lying on a mattress on the floor, with her throat cut. Then I saw prisoner holding Annie by the hair at her neck, and he cut the back of her throat with a knife, a pen knife, which I had seen him with before.*

Jane had also been awoken by the screams and she joined her brother. She said, 'He's murdering her! He's murdering her!'

Luckily for them, Callaghan seemed not to notice them. He dropped his knife, kicked over the table and then washed his hands, before leaving the house. Although Ann was flat upon the floor and quite still in death, their mother was still alive. She moved her arms and tried to speak, but no words came. She died about ten minutes later. The two children ran to fetch the neighbours, and found Mrs Blackmore and Mrs Stevens.

Callaghan was asked if he had anything to say, and he replied, 'No, I reserve my defence.' The jury returned a verdict of wilful murder.

Seven days later, there was another hearing. Callaghan, who again reserved his defence, was committed for trial at the Old Bailey and was asked if he had any witnesses, replied, 'I don't know whether there are any. How am I to know?'

Callaghan appeared at the Old Bailey on 30 June. Prior to his appearance, he had been examined by doctors Bastian and Scott. They considered that the accused man was insane and therefore not responsible for his appalling actions. The judge then stated that an order would have to be made committing Callaghan to Broadmoor. He was admitted on 7 July and died there, twenty years later, on 26 January 1917.

It would seem that the family, who were probably living on the breadline already, had additional financial problems because of Callaghan's residing with them. They had taken him in, doubtless out of their natural concern for him; he was ill and unemployed. But, as his sister was in charge of housekeeping matters, she found him rather a burden. Yet he probably expected more from her, as he was her brother and so the two were set on a collision course which, in view of his insanity, was set to prove fatal.

CHAPTER 16

An Appalling Family Murder in Deptford 1902

My God, what have I done? I have killed all my children . . .

Killing on a large scale is usually associated with serial killers who do not usually know their victims intimately; for example, Reginald Christie and Dr Harold Shipman. Domestic murders, which are far more common, tend to be on a smaller scale of blood letting. The case to be related here combines elements of both these types of crime; and it is the locality's single most bloody incident.

Frank Cavilla, variously described as an unemployed house decorator, paperhanger or painter, was the son of Spanish parents who had settled in Hertford. A journalist described him thus:

> *He is a good looking man, with a mass of black hair, dark expressive eyes, delicately chiselled nose and chin and a wavy, fair moustache, dressed in a much worn grey suit and wearing no collar.*

He had been married to Helena, an Englishwoman, who was a year younger, for sixteen years. Most of their married life had been lived in Peckham. However, in 1902, they were occupying three rooms on the ground floor of a house in Batavia Road, New Cross. They had four children. These were Frank, aged twelve, Walter, aged eight, Nellie, aged four, and Ernest, aged sixteen months. The two eldest children attended Nynehead Street Board School.

Evelyn Smith, a neighbour, described him as 'a steady man': 'never heard of any threats or disagreement of any kind. Never a quarrel.' Frederick Cavilla, one of his brothers, who was in the same line of business and resided in Peckham, had seen Frank recently, and remarked that the marriage was a happy one, saying: 'Frank always lived very happily with his wife; they were like two turtle doves'. He added that Cavilla did not drink, and was a quiet, inoffensive man, but in company could be very jolly and liked playing the banjo.

All Saints' Church and Institute (left), c.1905. London Borough of Lewisham

Despite this apparent domestic bliss, all was not well. They had once enjoyed a degree of affluence, but times had changed for the worse. Cavilla had worked for one Mr Beck, a builder, and had lived in a house owned by his employer. Unfortunately, Beck was killed in an accident and Cavilla and his family lost their house as well as his job. Although they found new lodgings, Cavilla was only able to find casual employment.

Thus the family was often living in poverty. Sometimes there was no food to eat or oil to burn. Elizabeth Ayres, Cavilla's mother-in-law, later said that 'they have often been in want' and this was confirmed by Evelyn Smith, who said 'they were very much in want for nearly twelve months'. She recalled her neighbour often complaining to her about lacking the necessities of life. They had even had to sell their piano to help make ends meet. Occasionally, neighbours would send anonymous food parcels to the family. Apart from Cavilla's being unemployed, there was illness in the family and a doctor was owed £2. Cavilla had suffered from influenza in the previous year and, according to his brother, 'has never been right since'. Although there had been no money to pay for a doctor, by early August 1902, he seemed to be getting better. They could have gone to the parish doctor, whose services were paid for out of the rates, not by the patient, but had chosen not to.

Cavilla's wife had not always enjoyed good mental health either. Shortly after her marriage, she arrived at her brother-in-law's business dressed in her wedding dress and acted oddly. Cavilla became worried as his wife's health worsened and became frightened to live with her. She spent nine months in an asylum, but appeared to be cured so was discharged. After the birth of her youngest child, she had again been absent, under care, for seven weeks.

There were various comments made about Cavilla's state of mind. Elizabeth Ayres said, 'since that time [August] his wife had said that he did not appear quite right. She was asked if she was afraid of him, and she replied, "No, he would not hurt me"'. Yet she also later recalled that Frank had told her that his father had been sharpening a knife and 'was going to kill them all'. The witness said that 'she had thought nothing of it'. This was because Cavilla was fond of his children and they were unafraid of him. Frederick Cavilla thought that his manner appeared strange and that he rambled. Apparently, he was convinced that people were after him and wanted to harm him.

However, all this was to change suddenly on Monday 2 September 1902. Apart from sounds of the baby crying until 4.00 pm, nothing was heard or seen of any of the family until the evening, and this was very unusual. At 1.00 pm a man called but received no reply. The two elder children had not attended school. Then Evelyn Smith began to hear sounds of someone pacing up and down. She also heard sounds of bitter crying. Then she heard Cavilla's voice. He said: 'My God, what have I done? I have killed my children.'

She became extremely nervous and worried and conferred with another neighbour about what she should do. Eventually they decided to summon help. Albert Kirby, the landlord's son, went for the police. It was 11.15 pm when they arrived at the Cavillas' home, and Cavilla answered the door. PC Moore asked to see his wife and children, if they were at home. He replied: 'Yes, they are in, and I will show you where they are.'

Before he could do so, he suggested that they put a penny in the gas meter slot in order to see anything within. This alone was a comment on their poverty. They then saw a shocking sight. As the local newspaper noted:

They found the bodies of the wife and the second child, aged eight, lying on the floor of the bedroom, and the other three children, two boys and a girl, on the bed. All were dead. The poor woman was dressed only in an undergarment, the child on the floor was fully dressed with the exception of his boots and the other children were in their night clothes. They had all met their deaths by having their throats cut with a large pocket knife, which was found on the mantelshelf. The room presented a dreadful appearance, blood being all over the floor. One of the dead woman's blouses had apparently been used to wipe the boards, it been soaked in blood.

Cavilla was in the kitchen and made no attempt to escape. Moore showed him the rooms in which the bodies lay, and his prisoner simply said, 'I did it.' When Detective Inspector Hailstone told him that he would be charged with the murder of his wife and children, he simply nodded his head and remained silent. Thinking that he did not understand the gravity of the charge, Hailstone repeated himself. Cavilla replied 'Yes', and then was searched; a second knife being found on his person. This was confiscated and Cavilla was then sent to Blackheath Road police station and formally charged. He made no reply. Although his outer garments showed no sign of what had happened, bloodstains were found on his shirt sleeves. This suggested he had committed the murders whilst only partially dressed. It seems probable that he killed his wife and the three older children early in the morning, when two of them were preparing to go to school, whilst the baby died in the afternoon.

On the following day, Cavilla was brought before Greenwich Magistrates' Court. Hailstone and Moore presented their evidence and explained exactly what they had found at the scene of the crime.

Batavia Road, 2006. The author

Cavilla retained a stolid demeanour throughout the hearing. On being asked if he had anything to ask Hailstone, he replied, 'No, none whatever.' The magistrate, Mr Baggallay, remanded Cavilla for seven days and he was detained at Brixton Prison.

The inquest was held on 4 September, at All Saints' Institute, Monson Road, Deptford, before Mr George Wyatt, the coroner. Mrs Ayres and Mrs Smith testified to Cavilla's character and the happy marriage that he and his wife enjoyed, despite their recent poverty. Mrs Smith described her experiences on the day of the murder. The medical evidence was presented. Dr Taylor, the police surgeon, said that death had been due, in each case, to haemorrhage from loss of blood. He said that the pocket knife, about three and a half inches long, which had been used, was not sharp, so a great deal of force would have had to have been employed. Another doctor stated that there was a wound on Mrs Cavilla's wrist, which was indicative of the fact that she must have struggled before she died. She had probably been the first to die. He thought it odd that no cries for help or screams were heard. Cavilla, once again, had nothing to say. The jury found a case of wilful murder against him, but added that 'they did not think the prisoner was answerable for his actions at the time'. At the trial at the Old Bailey, medical evidence was produced to show that Cavilla was unfit to plead and so he was sent to Broadmoor. He was admitted on 28 October 1902 and was discharged on 9 February 1920.

As there are no surviving medical reports about Cavilla, his exact mental condition is unclear. As his brothers later stated, they could only suppose that he had been suffering from hallucinations of persecution mania. He perhaps saw his family as the very enemies who were making his life a misery and so he sought to destroy them and so save himself. This, now, would most probably be diagnosed as paranoid schizophrenia; seeing things which were not there in reality. Jack London, in his study of London poverty at the beginning of the twentieth century, with reference to this tragedy, noted, 'misfortune and misery are very potent in turning peoples' heads, and drive one person to the lunatic asylum, and another to the morgue or the gallows'.

His victims must have suffered a few short moments of absolute horror and terror, when their once beloved father turned on them, killing them one by one, and none having a chance of escape. The scale of the shock and the dread can only be guessed at. As the newspaper headline described it, it was an 'appalling tragedy'.

CHAPTER 17

The Fingerprint which Caught the Killer 1905

If anyone asks if I was out last night, say, 'No, I was in bed' ...

T his murder is one of the best known in British criminal history, though not for the very ordinary victims or their killers. The murder of an old couple in Deptford in 1905 was as brutal a crime as any which stained the annals of history. It was, however, notable for one fact. It was the first time that finger-print evidence had been used in Britain to convict a killer. Had fingerprint evidence not been used, it is a moot point whether the guilty would have met their richly deserved fates.

George Chapman, who carried on a business in oils and paints – like the fictional Josiah Amberley in a Sherlock Holmes story set in Lewisham, a colourman – owned a number of shops throughout south-east London. There was one on Deptford High Street, which had been managed for three years by a now elderly couple, Thomas Farrow, and Anne, his wife, though they had been in Chapman's employ for twenty-six years. Chapman held Farrow in high esteem for his 'businesslike qualities and high character'.

On the morning of Monday 27 March 1905, young William Jones of Thames Street, Greenwich, who had been employed at the shop as an assistant for three years, turned up to work at 8.35 am, as usual. He later recalled:

I went to the shop, but was unable to get in ... I went to Mr Chapman's shop in London Street, Greenwich, and returned with Louis Kidman, who got in the back way and in the shop parlour found the body of Thomas Farrow.

Kidman sent Jones for the police.

A number of officers, headed by Chief Inspector Kitch, arrived on the scene. By now, rumours had spread that a violent crime had been committed, and a knot of spectators had gathered outside the shop.

Chapman's Oil Shop, Deptford High Street, 1905. London Borough of Lewisham

Farrow's body was found in the parlour near to the fireplace. His head had been terribly battered. The room was in a most disorderly state, suggesting that a struggle had taken place. Dr Francis Burney, the police surgeon, estimated that death might have taken place at about eight o'clock that morning. He thought that an instrument akin to a burglar's jemmy might have been used to kill the man.

They also found the body of Anne Farrow. She was lying unconscious on the bed upstairs. She was in her night clothes and there was a fracture at the base of her skull. She was not dead and, after her wounds had been dressed, she was taken to the Greenwich Hospital for Seamen, attended by two doctors. She was in a comatose state, but a policeman remained at her bedside in case she should regain consciousness and be able to give information about her assailants. Her situation was, however, critical and prospects for her recovery were not good.

The motive for the crime was soon obvious. George Chapman arrived at 9.30 am, as he did every Monday, to collect the week's takings. They usually amounted to between £14 and £15, although since that week's takings were missing, it was impossible to say exactly how much. The cash box was found to be empty and was carefully examined by the police and photographed – with crucial results. Another clue at the scene of the crime was the discovery of three black masks made from women's stockings.

After taking photographs of the interior and the exterior of the shop, the police made a statement. They had concluded that the criminals had obtained entry into the shop by trickery, for there were no signs of forced entry. They thought that at about 6.00 am, Farrow had been awoken and came downstairs in his trousers and waistcoat to see what the matter was. He opened the door and let the men in. Whilst he was attending to their needs, one of them struck him over the head with a blunt instrument. One of them then went upstairs and silenced Mrs Farrow in case she screamed and alerted passersby. Meanwhile Farrow put up a stout defence before he was killed. The thieves then ransacked the place in their search for the cash box, which they found under a mattress, and emptied it of money before leaving.

In the days immediately after the murder, the police arrested two men on suspicion. One was found at a lodging house and was detained at Bow Street Police Station until he was able to give a satisfactory account of his actions. Another man was taken in for questioning, but he was able to clear himself. The shop where the murder took place was open for business on the following day, but a police presence was needed in order to prevent any trouble by ghoulish souvenir hunters.

Meanwhile, the police had obtained a number of statements from witnesses who had seen two men in the High Street on the morning of the crime. Henry Alfred Jennings, a milkman and his lad, Edward Albert Russell, aged eleven, saw two men leave the shop and hurry down the street at 7.15 am. They left the door of the shop ajar and Edward mentioned this to them, at which one nodded to indicate that it was alright. They then walked off towards New Cross Road. One was in his late twenties, of medium height, had a round face and a medium moustache. He was said to be wearing a blue serge jacket, with its white collar turned up. He wore a hard felt hat. His companion was younger and a little shorter, with brown hair. He wore a shabby brown suit, grey cap and brown boots.

A barman of the Duke of Cambridge pub in the High Street claimed that there was a third man, who was about six feet high, powerfully built with a slight moustache. He wore a brown jacket, a bowler hat and a white shirt and collar, but lacked a tie. The three had arrived at about 6.00 am and spent about twenty minutes in the pub, drinking. The third man may have been one Henry Littlefield, who had nothing to do with the crime.

The inquest was held on 30 March, three days after the murder, at the Congregational Church Lecture Hall. The coroner stated that he hoped Mrs Farrow would recover in order to help bring the criminals to justice. Charles Farrow of Stanhope Street, Deptford, identified the corpse as that of his brother, who he had not seen for three years.

Duke of Cambridge, Deptford High Street. London Borough of Lewisham

Chapman reported that the shop usually opened at 7.30 am and would sell goods to painters who were on their way to work. Goods were delivered to the shop on Thursdays and Fridays, and cash was paid. Hence the takings would be low on those days.

Jones and Kidman then gave similar evidence about their discovery of the injured Mrs Farrow and the corpse of her husband. Police Sergeant Atkinson said that he found a sixpence and a penny on the bedroom floor, near to the empty cash box. He also stated that there was a bowl of water in which bloody hands had been washed and then wiped on a nearby white jacket. Dr Burney described the terrible nature of Mr Farrow's injuries. The skull had been fractured in several places. The murderer had used a great deal of strength. Death was due to a haemorrhage following the fracture of the skull. Although a jemmy was probably used, some of the wounds might have been caused by a hammer. The inquest was adjourned until 19 April.

Who was responsible? There was speculation in the local press. The men who had robbed a Lewisham jeweller in 1898 were accused, but they had been arrested and one was dead. A gang of London thieves, 'The Muffler Boys', was also accused. But the reality was simpler.

The police soon made two more arrests. On 2 April, at Greenwich Magistrates' Court, Alfred Stratton, a labourer, aged twenty-two, and Albert, his brother, a seaman, aged twenty, both living without fixed abodes in Deptford, were accused of being involved in the murder. They had been arrested the previous evening on the evidence of the witnesses who had seen them in the High Street just after the murder.

It was Police Sergeant Frank Beaver who found Alfred in the King of Prussia pub in Albany Street, Deptford. He said to him, 'Alfred, we want you.' 'What for? Poncing?' 'No.' 'I thought it was for living with Annie'. 'No. Where's your brother?'

'I haven't seen him for a long time, I think he has gone to sea.'

Alfred was taken to the Blackheath Road Police Station. He was found to have 18s 2½d on his person. Alfred asked Chief Inspector Frederick Fox,

> *What evidence have you against me?*
> *If you wish to know, I will tell you.*
> *I do wish to know.*
> *A milkman and his boy saw you and another come out of the shop door at a quarter past seven on Monday morning, and a young woman who knows you saw you and another man run across from the top of the High Street at Deptford towards Wilson Road.*

Alfred answered defiantly, 'I was in bed until 9.15 with Miss Ann Cromartie at 23 Brookmill Road.' Ann later gave evidence against

Mill Hill Lane, Brookmill Road, 1890s. London Borough of Lewisham

Alfred, with whom she had been living for about a year. On the day before the murder, Alfred 'got cross' and hit her twice. They had gone to bed at midnight, but Albert had knocked on the window in the early hours of the morning. Alfred said to Albert, 'Shall we go out tonight or leave it for another night?' The two brothers then left together and Alfred did not return until 9.15 am.

Inspector Arthur Hailstone arrested Albert in Deptford High Street. Hailstone later stated, 'He turned very pale and trembled violently.' When told of the charges, he merely answered, 'Is that all? Thanks.' He later said, 'If this comes to anything, I suppose we can have a solicitor.'

The two were placed with fourteen other men in an identity parade. Ellen Standon, who had seen the two in the High Street on the morning of the murder, was able to identify Alfred. The other witnesses were unable to identify either man. On a previous occasion, Albert Newton, who kept a coffee stall in the High Street, identified the two men. Both brothers were remanded in custody.

In the interim, Mrs Farrow died of her injuries. The inquest on 2 April stated that she had died on 31 March due to the effects of a fractured skull. Unfortunately, although she had briefly regained consciousness, she was unable to make a statement. The inquest was adjourned.

The Strattons were formally accused of the double murder and theft at Tower Bridge on 18 April. The police argued that the crime had been planned in order to take the maximum amount of money just before it was collected by Chapman on Monday morning. The evidence of another witness was given, who had seen the Strattons in the High Street that morning. Harry Littlefield, a professional boxer, saw them there at about 2.30 am (it is possible he later went for a drink with them and was seen with them in the Cambridge pub). Alfred had said to him, 'Hulloa, Harry, out again?' 'Yes. I have good reason for being out.'

The three walked down the street. Littlefield said he thought that Albert was fumbling with something under his coat. Alfred was wearing a brown suit, check cap and brown boots; Albert a dark blue serge suit and bowler hat. These descriptions tallied with those given by Jennings and his lad of the two men leaving the shop. Another witness, one Ellen Standon, said she saw Alfred running down the High Street towards New Cross. Her description tallied with that of the others. A Miss Compton had seen Alfred at about 2.30 am in the High Street with another man whom she did not know. They had had a brief conversation.

The evidence of the masks was next. Albert's landlady was a Mrs Tedman of Knott Street, and she said she found similar masks in his room. Kate Wade, who had lived with Albert, said that he had asked her about stockings to be used as masks. It was said that when Alfred returned home at nine o'clock that morning, his clothes smelt of paraffin, which was sold in the shop they had robbed. Alfred had told Ann that he had hidden 'four quid' near the pathway through the Kent waterworks. Alfred also told her that if she was asked, she was to say he had not been out. Alfred was suddenly flush with money, having been penniless on the previous day, and sent out a lad with money for food and fuel. Ann said that, after reading a description of the wanted men in a newspaper, Alfred got rid of his brown coat and blacked up his brown boots. Alfred Purfield, a painter, said he saw Farrow, who was very badly injured, briefly open the door of his shop at 7.25 am. Finally, a thumb print had been found on the cash box and it matched one of Alfred's.

The two brothers came before the Old Bailey on 5 May. Both pleaded not guilty. Richard Muir was prosecuting and he went through the evidence against the two men. He argued that Albert had called on Alfred at about 2.30 am and that the pair had gone to the shop. He told how Ann Cromartie had commented to Alfred, on reading about the murder, 'Is not that description like you?' Alfred replied, 'Do you think I would do such a thing and walk about the streets afterwards? Think how well known I am. If anyone asks if I was out last night, say "No, I was in bed".' Others who were in the same house recalled that Albert had called around for Alfred.

Muir also related a story told to him by a gaoler, who had spoken to Albert on 18 April. Albert asked him, 'How do you think I shall go on?' 'I don't know'. 'Is he listening?' asked Albert, indicating his brother's cell. The gaoler went to look and then replied, 'No, he's reading a newspaper.' Albert then decided to be remarkably frank,

> I reckon he will get strung up and I will get about ten years. He let me into this. He is the cause of my living with that woman. Don't say anything to him. I shan't say anything until I can see he has got no chance and then . . .

Albert continued:

> I don't want to get strung up. He has never done any work in his life except one month. They tried to get that Brixton job on him, but they found that he was at work at the time. I have only been out of the Navy about seven months.

Muir then went onto the crucial evidence of the fingerprint. He explained that no two human fingerprints are identical. After Alfred had been arrested, impressions were taken of his fingerprints. They were then compared to the print on the cash box and it matched that of his right thumb. There were twelve different points of similarity between the two.

It is worth noting that a Fingerprint Department had only been established at Scotland Yard as recently as 1895. It was the creation of Sir Edward Henry, Assistant Commissioner of the CID in London. The system was based on the fact that no two fingerprints are exactly the same. Although fingerprint identification had been used in a burglary case in Denmark Hill in 1902, it had never before been used as evidence in a murder trial. There were many who were sceptical and refused to admit its importance.

The trial continued and concluded on the following day. The case for the prosecution was coming to an end, but not before PC Gull told the court that two sovereigns and half a crown had been found wrapped in a piece of cloth near the waterworks by the Ravensbourne River, as Ann said it would. The key witnesses; Russell, Jennings, Littlefield, Standon, Purfield and Compton all gave their evidence again. Inspector Collins then discussed the fingerprint clue again. Collins explained that there were between 80,000 and 90,000 sets of prints at Scotland Yard. He had never found any to correspond. At the request of a juryman, Collins took a cast of his fingerprints in order to show the differences between them.

Speeches for the defence then began. Despite the evidence given by witnesses that he had been seen in the High Street on the morning of the murder, Alfred maintained that he had been in bed all of that time, though he did revise it a little. He also gave an alibi for his brother, by claiming Albert came to see him at about 2.00 am. Albert said he needed money for a room. Alfred opened the window and replied, 'I cannot spare any, but wait a minute and I'll slip you in here.' He got up, dressed and looked for his brother, who had walked off to Regent Street. It was here that they met Littlefield and Compton. At about 3.30 am the two brothers went back to Alfred's lodgings, so he said. They remained there until about 9.00 am.

Alfred explained that the paraffin was on his clothes because he had spilt some whilst filling a lamp. He said that he always told Ann to cover for him when he was out because he was always being accused of causing trouble. He said that they had never entered Farrow's shop and could not have been the men seen leaving there because they had been asleep until 9.00 am. He claimed that the cash he had buried had been buried before the murder and that he put it there because he feared he might spend it or it might be stolen from him and that he intended to give it to Ann. The money had been won at a boxing match over two months before.

Dr Garson, who claimed to be a fingerprint expert, said that the evidence was flawed. He pointed to the dissimilarities between the print on the box and Alfred's. He admitted that the two might be of the same person. Garson's veracity was put into question when a letter which he had written to the Director of Public Prosecutions was read out in court. In it, Garson had written:

I feel that the Government has, perhaps, the first claim on my services. I may say that if I am not retained by the Treasury as an expert, I shall probably give evidence as such for the defence, and that is the reason I am desirous of knowing as soon as possible whether my services are required by the Treasury.

Garson said in his defence that he was an independent witness. The judge said that he was 'An absolutely untrustworthy one, I should think, after writing two such letters'.

Mr Rooth, counsel for the defence said that he did not propose to call Albert as a witness. He now summed up. He said that Alfred was in bed at the time of the murder and that he wore a blue coat, not a brown one. He added that there were no bloodstains on his clothing. The money which had been buried had been his own and had been hidden for the reasons Alfred had already explained. He also said that Albert's remarks in gaol did not constitute evidence. Finally, he poured scorn on the fingerprint evidence, arguing that there were as many dissimilarities as similarities between the prints. Muir then summed up for the prosecution and the defence made the suggestion that the account of Albert's incriminating talk about his brother was inaccurate.

The judge then reminded the jury that these remarks could not be used as evidence and so should be ignored. He said that the strongest evidence in favour of the prisoners was that the two who saw the two men leave the shop could not identify them as being the two Strattons. He also argued that the fingerprint evidence was rather dubious. The jury took two hours to decide their verdict – an unusually long time.

They found the prisoners to be guilty of murder. Neither Stratton had any comment to make. The judge donned his black cap and, after the formalities, sentenced them to death. On their departure from court, Albert had a peculiar smile. Their mother fainted on hearing the news. They were executed at Wandsworth prison at 9.00 am on 23 May. The inquest following their deaths revealed that one had died instantaneously and the other had not, but there had been no feeling in his body at that time.

Fingerprint evidence had been important in the case, but was not by itself conclusive. The first murder case in which it alone was to prove conclusive took place four years later. Sceptics, both within the police and without, said that the system was a useless one, because in future all criminals would wear gloves. This has been proved to be fallacious by subsequent criminal history.

CHAPTER 18

A Crooked Councillor: Theophilus Williams 1908

I smelt a rat and consulted my colleague, and we reported the matter to the police ...

There is now a certain cynicism about elected councillors and local government in general among people today. It was not always so; Joseph Chamberlain in the late nineteenth century and Herbert Morrison in the early twentieth were seen as towering figures in that milieu. Yet there were rogues even then. One such was Lewisham's first (and possibly, worst) mayor. On one level, the rise of Theophilus Williams reads like a Victorian success story; from rags to riches. As a local newspaper observed: 'The career of the late Mr T.W. Williams was in many respects remarkable.' Yet Williams also possessed a shady side to his character, as shall be revealed.

Williams had humble origins – being born around 1843, the son of an East End tradesman. He came to Lewisham as a young man and secured the post of junior clerk in the Sydenham branch of the London and South Western Bank. He rose to the rank of manager, having been transferred to the Forest Hill branch. In 1874 he widened his interests and renown by becoming the Sunday School super-intendent at the Congregational Church in Sydenham. He also preached at open-air services. Although he was physically a small man, the dapper Williams had a compelling voice and was a natural orator.

Williams was tremendously ambitious. As well as elevating himself by progressing in his career and becoming well known in religious circles, he also bettered himself by marrying well. His choice was Miss Dexter, a wealthy Sydenham woman. With her money behind him, he was able to reside in a number of large properties, including Borrowdale in Sydenham, a house in Burgess Hill in Sussex and one at Morden Hill, Lewisham. The latter was partly financed by the fortune of Miss Dexter's sister, Esther, who lived with them.

Williams did possess a number of gifts which he made full use of. As the local newspaper noted:

At one time, Mr Williams was undoubtedly a man of wealth and to a certain degree was popular. He possessed the faculty of gathering colleagues around him. He had the art of influencing men and exciting and retaining their utmost confidence. If he made enemies he also made fast friends.

A contemporary, Anthony Runacres, said of his one-time employer: 'His was a dominating personality, he had tremendous charm and forcefulness and had built around himself a great reputation for public service.'

As a man of some wealth, Williams had no need to work in the bank, so he resigned and gave his time and energies to other matters. He bought a chain of newspapers including a local one, whose offices were in Deptford High Street. These allowed him a public mouthpiece and he freely used them to attack his enemies in print, though not without cost as he was sometimes 'mulcted in damages for libel'.

Williams entered politics in the 1870s. He was elected in 1876 as a member of the Lewisham Vestry and in 1882 was the chairman, remaining for many years. He was also chairman of the Lewisham Board of Works from 1882 to its dissolution in 1900, and was elected to the Metropolitan Board of Works for London, and later, its successor, the London County Council. Williams exerted considerable authority, especially in the Board of Works, where he was described as being at 'the height of his dictatorship'. He was also a Baths Commissioner and was on the Lewisham Parochial Charity Board. The only mild stain was being charged with illegal practices during an election in 1895 – using rooms above licensed premises for an election meeting. His career in local government reached its zenith in 1900 when he became first mayor of the new Borough of Lewisham, a post he unusually retained in the following year, during the Coronation of Edward VII.

In these roles, he did oversee a number of useful public projects. These included the building of the first gentlemen's public toilets in Lewisham, which stood at the north end of Lewisham High Street. There were a number of plaques to the memory of projects undertaken while he was at the helm of public matters, such as at the Town Hall and at the Central Library. On the other hand, he opposed projects such as the purchase of additional land for the cemetery in Hither Green Lane and for the tramway to be built through Lewisham. In these he was unsuccessful.

It was true that there were a few lapses in his public role. Once he was fined for acting as a vestryman without the proper qualifications

Theophilus Williams, 1900. London Borough of Lewisham

needed for that office. When he was mayor, he was granted a mayoral purse of an annual £300. This was of questionable legality at best. His colleagues were only able to escape their responsibility in the matter of an illegal vote by an appeal to the Local Government Board.

In 1902, Williams's luck turned. He had hoped for a knighthood during the period of Coronation honours (other mayors in London had been so honoured), but this was denied him. His popularity began to wane and there were stormy scenes in the council chambers in his second year as mayor. A year later, he abandoned public life. It was not until 1908 that he again emerged as a public figure, though in rather different circumstances.

It is now time to turn to Williams's private activities. With the fortune acquired by marriage and with the financial insights he thought he possessed from his banking career, he had begun to speculate on the Stock Exchange and did so in no small manner but with thousands of pounds. He even persuaded his employees to invest in his schemes. That he was so successful in convincing people of his financial astuteness was due to his having achieved such a respectable position in local society. Runacres recalled:

> He persuaded myself and another employee to invest some money in his ventures. I won't go into the technicalities but when I got my shares I smelt a rat and consulted my colleague and we reported the matter to the police. From there on matters took a natural course.

Runacres lost all his savings, but at least, at only twenty-one, he had time to make good his losses – others were not so lucky and lost all the money they had been saving for their old age. Another victim was a clergyman's widow with money, who Williams induced to allow him to invest her money in a manner which would yield ten times that which a bank would give her. He lost the lot. Williams was clearly a far from shrewd investor, or perhaps merely unlucky. Yet he thought otherwise. He promoted the Balla Balla Copper Company, which went bust and with it much of his own money. He ran through his wife's fortune and much of that of her sister. In all, he was thought to have lost £120,000 – a huge sum for the 1900s.

In order to try and cover his tracks, Williams had to live a double life. On one occasion, he pretended that he had a fictional brother, whose identity he adopted when it suited him. He also lived under the name of Lloyd and allegedly resided at Hythe in Kent. Ernest Graham was another of his aliases. He also had a number of addresses; one at Nigel Road and one at Osborn Road. Williams managed to cover his tracks to an extent by another method – by burning all his financial books and letters before they could be seen by official investigators.

The crash came in May 1908 as Williams was summoned to appear before the County Court at Lambeth to hear bankruptcy proceedings against him. Williams had drawn an income of £1,200 a year from his newspapers. He also claimed that the manager had been embezzling money. Although the latter was dead, his widow contested the allegation and Williams was forced to sign a letter that he had been taking the money, not the widow's late husband. When the court learnt that he had destroyed all his records, Williams said that he had been in a very distressed frame of mind at that time, so was not wholly responsible for his actions. He also said that he had been dealing with a man called Smith, who had been responsible for misusing his wife's money. Conveniently, this Smith, assuming he ever existed, was no more. He had, apparently, committed suicide.

Williams tried to avoid attending these court hearings. He decided to flee the country, but was arrested at the Great Eastern Hotel on Liverpool Street, en route for France, and brought to Brixton Prison. It was shown that he was planning to rent a house in France. Williams claimed he was merely following his doctor's advice and taking a sea voyage for his health, but a trip from Dover to Boulogne (which is what he had a ticket for) hardly seems to fit the description of a relaxing cruise. Yet it was true that he was a sick man – on one occasion when he did attend a court hearing, he had collapsed in a tram car on the Old Kent Road. Furthermore, to add to his distress, his wife had died.

Eventually Williams was granted bail and friends of his guaranteed he would not try and escape again. He was declared bankrupt, but his troubles were not over. He had to face summonses at the Greenwich Magistrates' Court for illegally incurring debts. Apparently in 1907, he had incurred a debt of £500 to one Walter Foster, and had also had done likewise for £130 from Runacres, as well as trying to obtain credit on false pretences. At this time, Williams was living as a lodger in a little terraced house in Forest Gate – how are the mighty fallen. It was a far cry from the carriages and servants he had enjoyed at Morden Hill.

It was here that Williams died on the morning of 4 November, in circumstances which, like so much of the rest of his life, are unclear. His landlady, Mary Osborn found him in his bed, dead. He had taken an overdose of morphia. There was a phial and a hypodermic syringe by the bedside. His nephew had spoken to him a few days previously and said that he did not think his uncle was suicidal. However, Mary Osborn said that Williams had talked to her of his bad health and his other worries. Although, at the inquest, the jury considered that he had taken the overdose during a temporary fit of insanity and so the death was suicide, the coroner said that this was merely a supposition and so recorded an open verdict of 'Death through an overdose of morphia'.

Williams was buried with his wife at Ilford Cemetery. Only relatives attended his internment. As Mr Hatton who was presiding over the proceedings against Williams remarked, 'Ah! There's an end to the matter!'

Williams's public respectability had been merely a mask for a man who gambled on a vast scale with other people's money – and lost. It was not 'rags to riches' but a morality tale about deceit and greed leading to a tragic, but well-earned, downfall. Williams had tried to keep one step ahead of his pursuers until the very last, although, as he should have known, this was just the last step on the road to disaster.

CHAPTER **19**

Under the Floor Boards 1908

They seemed to be a very happy couple ... always sane and reasonable ...

Most of the murders related in recent chapters took place in Deptford, rather than Lewisham. This crime was committed in Lewisham itself.

On the evening of Monday 16 November 1908, PC John Smith was on his beat. He saw one George Hume, a forty-year-old tailor of Loampit Hill. Hume had his young son with him, but seemed to be wandering aimlessly about, in part because he had been drinking heavily earlier that day. Smith asked Hume what he was doing. 'I'm going to give the little b**** a wash'. Smith replied, 'I'm a police officer and in my opinion you are not fit to take care of a child.'

Loampit Hill, c.1905. London Borough of Lewisham

Hume also told Smith that people in the street had been staring at him and making 'dumb motions' at him. Although Smith knew little of Hume, he was right in his opinion. The two of them were taken to the police station in Blackheath Road. Inspector Garner questioned him about the whereabouts of his wife. Hume said that she was in Cambridgeshire with her parents. Garner recalled, 'He seemed very strange in his manner.'

Hume was escorted to the Workhouse Infirmary on Lewisham High Street, where he would be treated. He was said to be certainly not in his right mind and was treated as being at least temporarily insane. On arrival, it was noted by John McArdell, an attendant, that he was 'very confused and smelt strongly of drink and made incoherent statements about the infidelity of his wife and the paternity of his child'. Hume was placed in the Lunacy Ward. McArdell found that Hume had his wife's rings in his possession.

However, this was not the end of the story. It was to have a more sinister turn. Three days after this incident took place, William Curtis, who was the father of twenty-seven-year-old Bertha, Hume's wife, came up to London from Cambridgeshire to see his daughter. Unfortunately, on going to their house, he could not find anyone at home. Mrs Charlotte Moss, Hume's sister, called around on the following day, and with the same result. Where was Bertha Hume?

Curtis decided to return to the house on the day following, with Hume's sister, and together they effected an entry. The house was partly used as Hume's workshop for his tailoring business. They noticed some clean cuts in the linoleum which covered the shop floor. Charlotte stood on a board which felt loose. Raising the linoleum, they saw that the boards underneath had also been cut. It was time to call the police.

Inspector Garner arrived at the house. The flooring was removed and a bicycle lamp shone around. This revealed, three feet below, the fully clothed body of Bertha Hume. She had been strangled, with a piece of string which had been tied tightly around her neck. There was some blood by her head. A brown hat was also found there, with two pins in it, twisted as if the hat had been wrenched off her head. The body was removed to the mortuary where Dr Robert Donnellan, the police surgeon, examined it. He said death had occurred on either the evening of 15 November or the morning of 16 November and had been caused by heart failure due to pressure on the neck by the cord. He noticed that there was a large wound on the right cheek, but was not certain if it had been inflicted before or after death. It could have been caused by a fall to the ground. Although he thought she had been attacked from behind, a struggle had taken place and he noted finger marks around the throat.

A little was known of the Humes. Hume had been born in Jedburgh, was initially a farm worker, but then enlisted in the King's Own Scottish Borderers in 1889, aged eighteen. His service was creditworthy enough, being promoted to Lance Corporal and serving in India, awarded a medal during the Relief of Chital and later serving in the South African War. Hume left the army in 1902 with a good character. He married and set up as a tailor in a shop on Hither Green Lane, moving to Loampit Hill as business had been bad. Although Bertha was rather younger than her husband, the marriage appeared to have been a happy one. As a neighbour, Fanny Wilcox later said: 'I never knew them to have any quarrels; they seemed to be a very happy pair ... always sane and reasonable'. Likewise Curtis reported that 'They seemed happy enough ... on good terms.'

On the day after the body was found, Inspector Hawkins and two detective sergeants visited the infirmary in order to meet Hume. Hawkins told Hume that he was going to arrest him for the murder of his wife. Hume replied:

I almost forgot all about it. If I had not been jealous of her it would not have happened; but I could not stand the disgrace. I knew I had done something, and I was going to give myself up.

At the magistrates' court, Hume took very little interest in the pro-ceedings. Witnesses came forth to give evidence. First was Mrs Wilcox. She recalled seeing Mrs Hume with her son on a push cart on Sunday 15 November. She greeted Mrs Hume, but the latter did not reply. On the following morning, she saw Hume sweeping his door step, which was not a usual sight. She made conversation, asking him how his wife was. Hume replied, 'She is rather poorly ... I have been to get her some medicine. I have given her some. She will be better bye and bye. She is lying down upstairs on the bed.'

Hume then contradicted himself and told Mrs Wilcox that his wife had gone away. Yet when another neighbour, Mrs Chaplin, asked Hume how his wife was, he reverted to the story he had told Mrs Wilcox.

Mrs Chaplin was the next to come forward and made a strange accusation. She said that Hume had been drunk on 13 November, and was making a noise with a bundle of carrots and some wood. On 16 November, she spoke to Hume. He told her that his wife was ill and on the bed. When asked if she could do anything for her, he replied, 'I want to tell you something.' But he did not continue, and took his son in the direction of Lewisham High Street. The court was then adjourned in order to await the results of the inquest.

Other pertinent evidence was given at the inquest. Garner and Mrs Moss spoke, then William Turnbull, a barman, related a conversation he had had with Hume on the afternoon of 15 November, presumably when Mrs Hume was still alive. Hume had asked him, after pointing at a second hand shop near Algernon Road, 'Do you think I can get a revolver?' Turnbull did not answer, but Hume went towards the shop.

Although Mrs Wilcox repeated her evidence, she did have an additional piece of news. On 16 November, she remembered that Hume had told her that one Mrs Hemsley had made a fearful mess in his workshop and he had had to clean up. He added, 'I doubled her up and threw her old brown hat with her.'

Mrs Chaplin was convinced that Hume had said Hemsley not Hume. Her husband reported that on the early morning of 16 November, he had heard hammering next door. Alice Smith, another neighbour, reported hearing similar noises at about quarter to seven that morning.

It is possible that the murder was premeditated. David Sterry said that, on the evening of 13 November, he had visited Hume in order to have a jacket repaired. He noticed that Hume was cutting a hole in the floor board. Hume complained about his wife, 'I've had no bloody tea today' 'How's that?' 'The bloody old woman's been out all the afternoon.' Soon afterwards, Mrs Hume arrived. She was in tears.

On 16 November, Sterry had seen Hume outside the Roebuck pub, and asked how the work on his jacket was progressing, and Hume answered him, 'No, I shall never do that. I've done my bloody lot in. Come in to the public house and have a drink and I'll tell you something that will surprise you.' Sterry declined.

Mrs Moss shed some light on Hume's motive for killing his wife. Hume thought his wife was having an affair. When asked about this, she had struck him and behaved 'like a mad woman'. He then decided that he could not bear the disgrace of being attacked by his own wife. The jury at the inquest decided that wilful murder had been committed by Hume and he was committed for trial at the Old Bailey.

Dr Scott told the court that Hume's mind was deluded and he was possessed with the belief that his wife had once tried to kill him by inserting glass into his pudding. Hume further believed that the manager of the Salisbury pub on the High Street was his child's father. Finally, Hume said his wife had accused him of sodomy with her. There was a complete absence of remorse or regret on his part whilst in prison. When Hume was sent to the Old Bailey, and charged before Mr Justice Grantham, he was found guilty but insane, so was ordered to be detained at Broadmoor. He was discharged eleven years later.

As with Cavilla (see Chapter 16), it would appear that Hume was suffering from paranoid schizophrenia, with his belief that his wife

The Roebuck, Lewisham, c.1910. London Borough of Lewisham

had betrayed him and wanted to kill him. Perhaps what made the tragedy worse was that it left a small lad (never named in the reports) bereft of his parents, and we do not know what his fate was. Perhaps the Curtises or the Mosses looked after him, as they were his next of kin.

CHAPTER 20

The Lewisham Murder
1919

I did it with a bar of iron ... I don't know why I did it ...

In 1919, John William Thomas Prickett (hereafter Prickett senior), a middle-aged carpenter, owned a house in Blagdon Road, Lewisham. He was a widower, and lived with his unmarried son, John George (hereafter Prickett), who had been an assistant clerk at Somerset House since 1910. Prickett was a quiet young man, who had enlisted in the Forces in the summer of 1918 and served for eight months in the Royal Field Artillery at Woolwich.

Prickett was demobilized in January 1919 and resumed work for his old employer. His sister, Florence, who was a hospital nurse in Bermondsey, did not live at home. The household also consisted of Priscilla Elizabeth Bacon, aged sixty-eight, and widow of Robert Bacon, who had been a printer at the East London Industrial School, Lewisham. She had rented a room there for two years, but was looked upon as one of the family, and was on good terms with Prickett, for whom she acted as a surrogate mother. It would seem that this was a fairly contented little household.

Yet tragedy was to befall it. Unfortunately Prickett had a history of illness. In 1916, he was unwell, having 'contracted a certain disease well known as a direct cause of insanity'. This may be a discreet allusion to a venereal disease, perhaps syphilis, for which he was treated. During most of his brief military service, he had been in various hospitals, suffering from influenza. Shortly after his discharge he had suffered from congestive headaches and had had an epileptic fit. After that he seemed better, and was back at work.

On 5 July 1919, he took a fortnight's holiday from his work. Although he had arranged to go to Brighton, he decided to cancel the booking at the last moment. On Sunday 20 July, the last day before he was due to return to work, he had breakfast, then returned to bed, feeling ill and complaining that his mind was wandering. When his sister Florence visited, she thought her brother 'seemed strange in his

Blagdon Road, 2006. The author

manner; he did not eat and had not washed himself'. His father suggested he should see a doctor. Prickett agreed and Dr Orr of Lewisham High Street saw him that evening. Orr said that the patient needed rest and nursing. He recommended a nursing home, but that would have been too expensive. Therefore, a stay in Greenwich Infirmary was the next best thing and an order from the relieving officer was obtained in order to facilitate this.

Prickett was in the infirmary from 23 July to 6 August. His father visited him twice and was told by the attendant that his son was bright and cheerful. Prickett left for home, paying his sister a visit at Bermondsey Military Infirmary on the way. He had a good dinner at home and then left on 8 August, not saying where he was going. He did not return on the following day and the police were notified. He had written to his sister to announce that he planned to end it all – by drowning in the river. His father walked the Thames Embankment for two hours, looking for his son, but without success.

On 9 August, a telegram addressed to Prickett senior arrived. It was from his daughter-in-law, who lived in Addiscombe. It read, 'Jack found at Sevenoaks. Harry gone down.' Harry Prickett was John's brother and was at Sevenoaks Police Station, where he was told that Prickett had been sent to Sundridge Infirmary after having attempted to commit the crime of suicide. Apparently Prickett had wandered about all night, waiting for the shops to open. When they did, he bought some sulphuric acid, which he consumed. After vomiting a great deal, he went to the police station to find the surgeon. At the infirmary, he announced that he was tired of life. Prickett was in great pain due to the effects of the acid he had swallowed, and could eat little.

Prickett was brought before the Sevenoaks magistrates and committed for trial for attempted suicide at Maidstone Assizes on 16 October. However, he was allowed bail, and his brother and sister-in-law returned him to his father's house. There had been some discussion as to whether he ought to have been detained by the police, or to have remained at the infirmary, but the consensus of opinion was that this was not necessary as, after conversation, Prickett seemed to be much better. Florence later noted, 'he seemed quite normal'.

In any case, he could not remain at the infirmary, and the police did not want to hold him. He therefore returned home. On 20 August he shook Mrs Bacon warmly by the hand. Prickett retired to bed at 10.30 pm. His father remained downstairs, talking to Mrs Bacon, before she retired too. On the morning of the following day, Prickett senior left home for work.

When he returned home, it was about 6.10 pm. He opened the front door, went through the passage and passed by the kitchen door. It was then that he noticed something was amiss. On the oilskin on the floor just in front of the kitchen door, there was a pool of water. Presumably the water had been left running and had overflowed onto the floor. Removing his coat, he went upstairs to the bathroom and opened the door. He then saw a shocking sight.

There was a body in the bath. It was of a fully dressed woman, who was lying on her right-hand side and her left cheek was just above the water. The bath was three-quarters full and was bloodstained. He put her hands under her chin and moved the face around. It was Mrs Bacon.

He searched the house for his son. He was nowhere to be found. There had been no sign of any struggle and the house was perfectly in order. He then planned to send a telegram to his son-in-law in Croydon. Before he could do anything, he found that there were policemen at the front door. They had arrived as Prickett had given himself up to them. At 5.30 pm, Prickett had told Sergeant William Tissington,

I want to give myself up for killing a woman . . . Mrs Bacon, aged sixty . . . I struck her on the head with a piece of iron. I then drowned her in the bath in the house, I don't know why I did it I'm sure. This happened at two o'clock.

Detective Inspector James Pulle was in charge of the investigation. The corpse was removed to a bedroom and examined. There were bruises over the left eye, on the nose, the right side of the neck and on the back of the right hand. There was also a wound on the back of the neck. The hair was undressed and wet. In the bathroom, bloodstains were found on the washstand, mirror and bath. There were further marks on the bathroom wall, some as high as five feet. The floor was saturated with water and there was a hair comb and hair pins there.

Prickett was at Blackheath Road Police Station. Pulle verified his identity and told him he would be charged with Mrs Bacon's murder. He then cautioned the prisoner, who asked: 'Is my father there? Is my sister there?' Pulle told him that they were. Prickett then confessed. 'I did it with a bar of iron. You will find it on a rack in the kitchen. I don't know why I did it.'

Pulle found the murder weapon – to which hair was attached. Prickett's shirt had bloodstains on the right shoulder. On the day after the discovery of the murder, Prickett was formally charged at Greenwich Magistrates' Court. Pulle related his evidence and Prickett was then sent to prison.

The inquest was held on Monday 25 August. Prickett had chosen not to attend. Frederick Samuel Bacon, a young clerk of Deptford, identified the corpse of his mother. He said that his mother had always spoken well of Prickett. However, he said that his mother had been tending Prickett when he had been unwell in February, suffering from delusions. Apparently, the delirious Prickett had told her at this time, 'I will do for you and kill myself afterwards.' Mrs Bacon had later told her son, 'I am not a bit afraid of him.' Her son had suggested that she should live with him instead, but she refused. Evidence was also heard from Prickett senior about his son's recent history and his discovery of the corpse.

Dr Donnellan, the Lewisham police surgeon, had carried out a post-mortem examination of the corpse and made his report. He told the court of the nature of Mrs Bacon's injuries, but said that she had not drowned, nor was her skull broken. Instead, she had died due to passive suffocation, because of her unconscious condition. The latter had been caused by the blows to her head. She had then been taken to the bath and put in it, before being held under the water by her throat. He did not think it was useful to discuss Prickett's mental condition. The jury found that Mrs Bacon had been murdered by Prickett and that he should be tried for the crime.

On 10 September, Prickett was put on trial at the Old Bailey. Sir Richard Muir, prosecuting, said that he believed Prickett was insane and so unable to instruct counsel for his defence. Dr Griffiths, medical officer at Brixton Prison, concurred. He had interviewed

Prickett, had observed him on a number of occasions and had read the reports about him. When he had first seen Prickett, he said that he had been 'in a nervous and agitated state and suffering from deep mental depression'. Apparently, he took no interest in his fate and said he had to kill someone so he would be hanged, as he had been unsuccessful in his previous suicide bid. He added:

> his present mental condition ... is one of deep depression ... un-interested in the act he is charged with committing, but appears obsessed with his mental misery and the necessity for the ending of his life.

Prickett apparently spoke 'in a dull monotonous tone' and it was said he 'was insane at the time of the commission of the alleged act'.

Ironically, relations between the deceased and her killer had been excellent, and he had said of Mrs Bacon, 'She was a very nice old woman. I used to go to church with her.' Florence said, 'My brother and Mrs Bacon were on very affectionate terms.' The feeling was reciprocated as Prickett senior observed, 'She often spoke of John George Prickett, she had a great respect for him.'

The jury found that Prickett was indeed insane and so could not be tried. Mr Justice Roche, the judge, ordered that Prickett be sent to Broadmoor, where he was admitted on 18 September.

Presumably Prickett became suicidal because of his frequent illnesses. Having failed to commit suicide, he killed in order to receive the death sentence. Yet as he was found insane and incapable of pleading for his life, he had failed yet again. Perhaps this was punishment enough and poetic justice for his taking the life of a harmless old woman.

Interestingly enough, Prickett's father continued to live in the house on Blagdon Road until at least 1927. Perhaps it was difficult to sell, but the house's associations must have been morbid. Yet on 18 June 1930 his son was discharged, having recovered from the madness which had made him kill.

CHAPTER 21

A Soldier's Crime
1926

I have just seen the body of a woman at present unknown in the mortuary ...

At least two men were to have shocking experiences early on the Friday afternoon of 18 June 1926. The first was William Savage, an elderly man who was planting cauliflowers in a field on Shepherd's Farm, Catford. He heard agonizing screams and then saw a woman, 'bleeding profusely from several wounds, stagger through the gate into the field in which he was at work and collapse after going a few steps'. Others in the neighbourhood, including workmen at the Downham estate, rushed to the scene. Attempts were made to staunch her wounds and an ambulance was summoned from Lewisham Hospital, but it was too late, even if skilled medical attention had been immediately available.

The focus of the drama then shifted towards Arthur Staunton, who drove delivery vans for the Lewisham branch of Sainsbury's and who was driving along Verdant Lane, Catford. He was probably surprised to be hailed by a hatless young man who seemed terribly agitated, and he stopped his van. The young man asked: 'Where is the nearest police station? Will you drive me to the nearest police station?' Staunton replied 'Jump in and I'll see what I can do for you'.

The young man sat beside him in the van and they began to move off. Staunton asked him what was the matter. His blood pressure probably rose when the young man answered.

> *I have stabbed a woman. There's a police sergeant with her now, but I have dodged him so that I would not have to be walked through the streets. This will be something for them to buy* The Kentish Mercury *for!*
> *Was it an accident?*
> *Don't you understand me? I have stabbed a girl.*

After this dramatic exchange, the young man began to discuss the state of the weather and smoked a cigarette. Staunton later admitted that he did not fancy discussing the weather. He noted there was some

Verdant Lane, c.1920s. London Borough of Lewisham

blood on the man's right hand – clearly he had been wounded. He drove his passenger to the police station, where the latter thanked Staunton, walked in and gave himself up to the police.

Shortly afterwards, Police Sergeant Campbell arrived and identified him as the man who had run past him earlier that afternoon. Campbell had been walking along Whitefoot Lane when the young man had run towards him and said: 'There has been an accident up at the top; I'm going for the doctor.' Campbell had tried to stop him in order to elicit further information, but the man escaped into the undergrowth and disappeared. Detective Sergeant Davies heard the young man's story and told him he would be detained. Two more detectives arrived, including Detective Inspector George Hider, who took control of the case and went to inspect the corpse at Lewisham Mortuary. He saw there were four wounds on the back of the body, three on the chest and shoulders and one on the scalp. All these were caused by a knife. Dr Humphrey Nockolds said these eight wounds were 'of considerable violence'. Armed with these facts, Hider returned to the police station and told his prisoner, 'I have just seen the dead body of a woman at present unknown at the mortuary. You will be later charged with causing her death.'

The prisoner then made the following statement, after having been cautioned:

> *Yes, I know. I slept out all last night in the field, and only had one penny on me. I woke up early this morning and walked about until I saw the woman in the lane. I followed her and struck her in the back with a hunting knife. She screamed, so I put my hand over her mouth to stop her. I hit her again with the knife; I stabbed her in the front as she fell. I don't know what came over me. I threw the knife in the hedge and her handbag amongst some bushes in Whitefoot Lane. If you take me there I will point out where I threw them away.*

The police then went with their prisoner to the scene of the crime. He was William George Udall, a nineteen year old who was a private in the Royal Artillery. His parents lived at Minard Road, Catford. He showed the police where he had thrown away the murder weapon – a seven-inch hunting knife – and also the dead woman's handbag, which he had taken from her.

There were dry bloodstains on the knife. However, the contents of the handbag were more interesting. It contained letters which enabled the corpse to be identified as Mrs Ethel Hartley, who was twenty-seven and currently residing at Southend Lane. She was known as Ethel Hall, because she was separated (amicably) from her husband, James William Hartley, a shipping clerk of Leahurst Road.

Udall was brought before Greenwich Magistrates' Court on the following day. He was described in the local newspaper as:

> *About five feet ten inches in height, of soldierly bearing, he has refined and intelligent features. The firmness which at the outset of the brief proceedings marked his demeanour was later less apparent, and at the close he was obviously labouring under strong emotion.*

Hider told the court about the evidence of the knife, Udall's statement and the identity of the woman. The Clerk of the Court asked Udall if he had any questions. He had not. Hider asked the clerk if an order could be made to send Udall to prison, and this was granted.

More information was forthcoming at the inquest which was held on 22 June. Udall retained his usual cool exterior: 'He maintained a perfectly calm demeanour throughout, and even when giving evidence betrayed no sign of distress.'

Southend Lane, c.1914. London Borough of Lewisham

The first witness to be called was the widower, James Hartley. He told how he and the deceased had been married in 1920 and lived together for two years. His wife had then taken a variety of jobs, presumably as a servant, in Kent, Manchester, Ealing and finally Sydenham. They had been separated since about 1922, yet remained on friendly terms, seeing each other occasionally and he supplied her with money. At the time of her death she was working at Dulwich. She had reverted to her maiden name because she found it easier to find employment. He added, in answer to a question from the coroner, 'he was certain she led a perfectly moral life'.

Amelia Gould, with whom the deceased had lodged, recalled that she was 'a nice cheerful girl'. On the Friday of her death, she remembered being told that Ethel was going to have lunch at Williamson's restaurant in Catford and then visit a friend in Forest Hill, before returning home for tea.

William Savage, who had witnessed her death, recalled that he had seen Udall and her struggling at the edge of the Forster Memorial Park. He recalled approaching her and telling Sergeant Campbell that he had seen her assailant in flight. Campbell then recounted his evidence, as did Staunton.

Hider then gave a little of Udall's life story. He had been born in 1907 and left school in 1922. Udall initially worked as an assistant warehouseman in a City firm, where he was responsible for a number of other workers. However, he did not get on well with them and so left the job in 1924. He then briefly worked as a travelling salesman, before joining the army in 1925. Udall was serving at Bordon Camp, which he left on 9 June in order to see his mother.

Once back at home, his mother advised him to return to the army. He refused, saying he would only go when called for. Eventually he left home, a week later, planning to return to the army, but became fearful as to what the consequences might be. So he walked to Chiselhurst and spent the night of 16 June on the Common. Udall returned to Catford on the following day, but only had a penny, so slept in a hedge and wandered about in the vicinity of Whitefoot Lane in the morning of that fateful day.

It was at about 2.30 pm that he had seen Mrs Hartley. He told the court:

> *I did not know who she was and had not seen her before. I followed her for a short distance, and then a desire came over me to kill her; for what reason I do not know … I did not speak to the woman and had no intention of doing her any harm, but giving way to my feelings for the moment I drew my knife and struck at her blindly.*

During the attack, Mrs Hartley bit Udall's hand when he tried to stifle her screams. In the court, Udall was very apologetic,

> *I am extremely sorry that this has happened. I do not know what came over me, but I had a desire to kill and the same thing might have happened to any person that got in my way that moment.*

Minard Road, c.1905. London Borough of Lewisham

He also asked, if Mrs Hartley was going to Forest Hill, why was she walking up Whitefoot Lane, which did not lead there, but this question was not deemed to be appropriate.

The coroner then summed up the evidence. He suggested the motive for the attack by the almost penniless Udall was the hope that the woman's handbag might contain £5 or even £10, not just 9d. He then told the court that Udall might have killed anyone, 'It might have been your own daughter or your own wife . . . A more horrible state of things one cannot imagine.' The jury did not need any discussion to decide on what was the only possible verdict – that Mrs Hartley was murdered by William Udall. He was then told he would be tried at the Old Bailey for murder.

Udall's trial took place in the following month. As expected, much of the evidence which had already been given at the magistrates' and the coroner's courts was given again. Udall initially pleaded 'guilty', but quickly changed his plea to that of 'not guilty'. The prosecution outlined the known facts leading up to the murder, and called the witnesses to support this case.

The defence was that of insanity and the chief evidence for this was that given by Udall's parents. Udall had suffered a mental blow in 1924 when a girl had broken off her 'association' with him. From that time on, he became increasingly morbid, sitting for hours doing nothing and being moody. He had even attempted to take his own life. During his working life, he felt that his colleagues were laughing at him.

Udall's parents supported this belief. They added that the knife had been bought by their son for self-defence in 1924 and he usually hid it under his pillow. However, in an early deposition, Udall said 'I bought it as I intended to kill a girl with it after she threw me up but my people hid it away and I could not find it until now.' A distant relation had died in an asylum and another was said to be 'very funny in her ways'. Dr Beckel said that Udall was 'mentally abnormal' and that Udall often walked in his sleep and, enigmatically, had 'been living an abnormal sexual life', although no evidence was given to elaborate on this point. However, Dr Watson, doctor at Brixton Prison, claimed that Udall was not insane. It is a pity that the full medical report which a doctor would normally compile in the case of a prisoner who was deemed insane does not survive.

What is odd is that there is no reference to his military service. He was an army deserter and yet there seems to have been no statement from his commanding officer. Perhaps the papers are missing, as surely the police would have made enquiries as to this matter.

In the summing up, the prosecution argued that, if Udall was deemed insane, then no one was sane. The judge, Mr Justice Branson, said that the question was not whether Udall had committed murder, as he patently had, but whether he both knew what it was he was doing and that he knew it was wrong. Was Udall guilty of murder but insane, or simply guilty? The jury did not take long to decide that the former verdict was correct. Udall's life had been saved, but he was to be sent to Broadmoor. He was admitted on 3 August. The treatment he received enabled him to recover and so he was discharged on 22 December 1935.

CHAPTER 22

The Solution to the Murder of Louisa Steele
1931

I saw the girl coming towards me ... when she passed me ... I turned around and caught her by the throat ...

Louisa Maud Steele was an eighteen-year-old girl in domestic service in Lee in 1931, like many others. What made her unusual was the manner of her death. Virginia Woolf commented in her diary for 26 January 1931 that there had been 'A Ripper murder on Blackheath'. Except that Louisa was not a prostitute, nor was her throat cut and it did not appear that a serial killer was at work. Her body was, however, mutilated and she had been killed by an unknown man for no apparent reason (which were features of the Ripper murders and which were noted by the press).

Louisa had worked for Miss Mabel Andrews, a professor of music, in Lee Road, Blackheath, for two years. On the evening of Thursday 22 January 1931, after enjoying a hearty meal, she left her employer's house for what was to be the final time. It was about 7.50 pm. She crossed the street to visit a friend of her employer, Miss Florence Collins, to return a book which she had borrowed. She then left to visit Butcher, Curnow & Co., a chemist's shop, on Tranquil Vale, Blackheath, in order to buy some syrup of senna. No one is known to have seen her alive after that, except for her killer. It was usual for her to return home by 9.00 pm, though she was allowed to stay out until 10.00. This night was cold and blustery, not a night on which to linger in the cold. By 11.00, her employer had become very worried as Louisa had never been out so late before. Miss Andrew's sister then reported the missing girl at Blackheath Police Station.

In the early hours of the following day, Louisa's corpse was found by Leslie Hall, a lamplighter employed by the South Metropolitan Gas Company, who was on his rounds, putting out the gas lights on the Heath. At 6.30 am, when he was extinguishing the lights on the

Louisa Maud Steele, 1930. Metropolitan Police

south-east end of the Heath, he noticed a black coat covering what turned out to be Louisa's almost naked body. The corpse was in that triangle of the Heath bordered by Shooter's Hill Road to the north, Prince Charles Road to the west and the Prince of Wales Road to the east. Hall called a passing cyclist, Laurence Harvey, who went to fetch a policeman. At about 7.00 am, PC Fripp was on the scene.

Lee Road, 1930s. London Borough of Lewisham

His superiors were not long in arriving. Louisa's body was naked except for her right stocking. Some of her clothes, though not all, were found nearby. The coat covering her was her own. It was also noticed that the heel of the right shoe was in the dead girl's left hand. There was no sign of a struggle in the immediate vicinity of the corpse. Superintendent Cooper of Scotland Yard was called to investigate. Sir Bernard Spilsbury, an eminent Home Office pathologist, was summoned to discover the cause of death.

For the first time in its history, the Yard made an appeal via the cinemas in the locality of Blackheath, including, no doubt, the Lee Imperial Picture Palace. The cinema was, after all, the mass medium of visual communication before the advent of television. Photographs of the girl were shown, together with an appeal for any information concerning her. There was also a great deal of press coverage in both national and local newspapers.

The police also issued another two requests. The first was to tell the public of two other incidents on the evening of the murder. There had been two non-lethal attacks on women in the locality: namely Miss Minnie Staunton in Manor Park, Lee, and Mrs Martha Holmes in Granville Park, Lewisham (neither too far from Blackheath). The assailant was described as:

Aged about twenty-eight, about five feet ten inches in height, medium build, loose limbed, probable weight about thirteen stone, dressed in a dark overcoat and dark cap, pulled slightly over eyes.

He had a slouching gait and shoes which enabled him to approach his victims silently. It seems as if this attacker was the killer because he did not try and snatch the women's handbags, but rather tried to strangle them. It was thought that a man of this description was missing from home and the fact had gone unreported, as the police had scrutinized all missing persons files in the South-East of the previous month.

Anyone who had witnessed these attacks or had seen any suspicious person loitering in these streets was urged to report this. Secondly, anyone who had witnessed anyone loitering around Blackheath between 7.45 and 9.00 pm on the same night was asked to help the police investigation.

Another woman later came forward to report that she had relevant information. Miss Ethel Chinnicke had been delivering church leaflets and had seen a man just before she found that Mrs Holmes had been attacked nearby. She confirmed much of the description already given.

One of the problems which hampered the investigation was that hardly anyone knew Louisa well. She had few friends or acquaintances. Her mother told the police:

> her daughter was not of the type who would enter into any casual conversation with any stranger who approached her ... [she was] *a girl of irreproachable character who would be the first to resent, forcibly if necessary, the unwelcome approaches of anyone who might attempt to push his undesirable company upon her ... So far as can be known, she was a girl without any of the romances which might be expected in one of her age, and was without any male friends with whom she could be said to have formed a particularly close acquaintanceship.*

She was said to be antipathetic towards young men, especially those of her own class. But if Louisa had few friends, thousands turned out for the funeral at Plumstead Cemetery. Police were needed for crowd control. George Steele, a labourer of Ann Street, Plumstead, and Louisa's father, had to be supported by two others to prevent his collapsing, such was the emotion he was feeling. The crowd was sympathetic – there were over fifty cards and floral tributes to the dead girl. These were from local organizations, such as Burrage Road Girls' school, which Louisa had attended, and the Woolwich branch of the British Legion, as well as friends and neighbours.

The public came forward to help the police in their request for information. One man was questioned at Blackheath, but was released several hours later. Another possible clue was a bloodstained piece of underwear found shortly after the murder in a railway cutting near Catford Station. It was thought that this might have belonged to the

Tranquil Vale, Blackheath Village.

Tranquil Vale, 1930s. London Borough of Lewisham

deceased. Perhaps of more significance, a man with bloody hands was seen at a coffee stall in Catford at about ten o'clock on the night of the murder. It would have been easy to travel from Blackheath by any of the four buses which ran through the Heath towards Catford. But it was not known where he went next and who he was.

One Owen Williams came forward to say that he had seen a woman answering Louisa's description sitting on a bench on the Heath at about 9.00 pm. She was with a man and was crying. When he walked over towards them, the man on the bench became very annoyed at the intrusion. He got up from the bench and wanted to know the reason for the intervention. Then the girl said to him, 'Come back Jack; leave him alone.' The only description of the man was that he had 'a twisted lip'. It is odd that this should have been used, because a Sherlock Holmes short story, *The Man with the Twisted Lip*, was partly set at a nearby location, at the Cedars, Lee. The police later found a piece of paper in the dead girl's room addressed 'Dear Jack', but there was no clue as to who Jack was or how she was connected with him. However, the description of the possible killer as given by the two women who were attacked earlier that night was given precedence over this description.

Another witness who was sought was a young man who had been with a girl on the Heath on a seat near to where the body was discovered on the night of the murder. Many people reported seeing them, but initial police enquiries failed to locate him.

Hundreds of statements were taken. Two days after the murder, two builders caught a bus from Lewisham to Stepney. They said they noticed a man get on the bus at Blackheath who fitted the description of the wanted man. He got off at the London side of Sheerness. Police attempts to trace him failed. Another man arrived at the police station to say that he had just seen the man on the Heath, though when the detectives arrived he had gone. People who had traversed the Heath on the night of the murder said that they did not notice anything untoward, but police concluded that a body lying under a coat would be very easy to pass by, especially on a dark and stormy night.

By the time two weeks had elapsed since the murder, over 2,000 statements had been taken (none of these now survive). Some had been volunteered by the public. Others had been the result of extensive door-to-door questioning. All the houses in Granville Park, Manor Park, Lee Road and Blackheath Village had been visited by the police.

Two confessions were made. One was by an inmate of an asylum in Romford. The other was by a man who was not local, but who was well acquainted with the details of the crime. He was questioned, but it was realized on the following day that all his information came from the newspapers so he was released.

Another red herring was an anonymous note found in a Southern railway carriage. It warned the police to watch Ladywell Recreation

Blackheath, 1920s. London Borough of Lewisham

BLACKHEATH, KIDBROOK CHURCH AND SHOOTERS HILL IN DISTANCE.

Ground for there would be another corpse found there. The police did as suggested, but nothing material happened. A man was arrested nearby, but that was as the result of another enquiry.

One suspect was arrested on 25 January and an identity parade was formed. The women who had been attacked on 22 January were summoned to try and pick him out. They failed to do so and so he was released out of the back door of the police station – such was the interest aroused by the murder, a large crowd had gathered outside the main entrance. This man was Donald Bradshaw, an unkempt man known to be violent, who could give no account of his activities on the night in question and was uncooperative towards the police. He was suffering from a paranoia complex and was committed to an asylum. Another suspect was Francis Farrell, a former policeman, who had once assaulted a woman, but his wife said he was at home on the night of the murder. Herbert Wattins of Woolwich, described as 'a moral pervert', was briefly suspected, but was also cleared. Yet another shady (and unidentified) character was seen running from Aberdeen Terrace towards Granville Park between 9.30 and 10.00 that night.

A suspect, who was never named, was believed to have been on the Heath on the night of the murder and to have been there on the following night, too. He had previously been in a mental institution, but there had been disagreement about the nature of his illness and he was eventually released. He was an educated man and had once served in the army; and was now living on an army pension. Although once found guilty of committing a minor offence, it was believed he was a homicidal maniac.

The inquest was held on the morning of Tuesday 27 January. The courtroom was packed, mostly with women. George Steele was the first to give evidence. As might be imagined, he was distressed, though trying to control his emotion. He identified the corpse and confirmed basic details about his daughter, He then told how he last saw her alive on the Wednesday, the day before the murder. It had been Louisa's half holiday. She had seemed normal enough and had left them to go to the cinema at Woolwich, before returning to her place of employment.

Miss Andrews was the next witness. She recounted how she had warned her employee about walking on the Heath or on any sidewalks. Most of her evidence was negative. She believed her a good servant of good character, who was perfectly contented. She knew of no reason why she should have stayed out and knew of no male acquaintances. The police had been called so soon because she had feared an accident might have befallen Louisa, who was usually so punctual in returning home. She added that Louisa could not have known she would have been leaving the house that evening, because Miss Andrew's brother was coming to supper and so she could not have made any plans to meet anyone that evening.

Leslie Hall spoke next about his finding the corpse. She had been lying on her back, with her right leg bent. He saw her bare head and one arm protruding from the coat which covered the rest of her. He added that the coat was soaking wet, as one would imagine it would have been after the rain of the previous night. He said he stayed with the corpse until the cyclist brought the police along.

Dr Knight, the deputy coroner, decided at this point to adjourn the inquest in order that more evidence and information could be gathered in.

The locality was in an uproar over the murder. Mr A J Morgan advertised judo classes so that women could learn to defend themselves. The East Lewisham Women Citizens' association urged that parks and open spaces be properly patrolled by the police. They also argued that more women police were necessary. *The Kentish Mercury* ran a series of articles by a self-defence instructor in ju-jitsu, in order to try and reassure female readers. This, if 'properly learned, involves no danger to the person using it, but is fraught with the possibility of serious consequences to the person who is its victim'.

The press were full of suggestions. Motor patrols should in future be used on the Heath and on other open spaces. The police should be given special powers to observe suspects. One reporter noted that elderly spinsters began to live in terror of being murdered in their homes. One wrote:

> *I was interested to reflect on the strange psychological fact that the less qualifications that certain elderly spinster possess for attracting the attentions of a murderer, the more they are prone to suffer a morbid anticipation of early assassination.*

Viscountess Astor raised the issue in Parliament on 5 February. She called for the appointment of women police officers for the greater protection of women and children on Blackheath. She also asked about public safety on other lonely stretches of land in London. One MP suggested that if the police were on horseback or in cars they could patrol such places with greater ease.

The adjourned inquest was held at Greenwich Coroner's Court on 17 February. The medical evidence was given first. Spilsbury reported that there were numerous injuries to the face; the right bone of the nose was fractured and there was bruising elsewhere on the face. These injuries had been inflicted after death, by blows and kicks whilst the body was on the ground. Her breasts had also been mutilated. These injuries were probably inflicted on the Heath as pools of blood were found nearby. There was no sign of any sexual assault.

The cause of death, however, was strangulation. Spilsbury said:

In my opinion, the girl was attacked from behind and the neck of the dress was drawn forcibly backwards, while counter pressure was made on the back of the head and neck.

Louisa would not have been able to cry out and would have lost consciousness after a few seconds, so would not have been able to have offered much resistance after the attack had commenced. The time of death was approximately 9.00 pm.

Then four witnesses were called. The first of these was Miss Andrews. She recounted much of what she had said at the first inquest. Florence Collins was called next, but again had little to report. She told how she had not seen anyone loitering outside her house when Louisa left, and had closed the door as soon as the two had parted. Thomas Cleeve, of Butcher, Curnow & Co., reported that he had shut up shop just before 8.00 pm. His assistant, who lived on the premises, recalled that no one had called there after that time on the night in question.

Finally there was the young man who had been seen with a girl near to where the body was found. He was Sydney Forsdike, a clerk who lived in New Cross. He and Miss Rose Sanderson, his girlfriend, had sat on a bench near Shooter's Hill road, Blackheath, on the night of the murder, from about 8.15 to 9.00 pm. They then left and walked towards Greenwich. On their journey, he had noticed something on the grass, which had looked like a couple on the ground. There was no movement, but a black coat seemed to be covering something, and he could see something like a head sticking out of it. Neither of them had heard any sign of a scuffle taking place. They made no closer investigation and on the following day Rose asked him if it might have been the corpse.

Louisa's past was investigated. Again, only a blank was drawn. She seemed to have led a blameless, if friendless life, and there was no indication that she had a boyfriend. This was stressed – as if there was a suggestion that, for some, the inquiry was as much about Louisa's morals as about her murder.

The jury did not need to discuss the case – they brought in the only verdict they could – murder by strangulation by person or persons unknown. Louise's father's sense of loss had also become one of outrage and even anger as he said, 'I want to meet the man and hope I will do so.' He then walked slowly out of the hall, eventually followed by the others.

By July, there were renewed attempts made to solve the case. Fresh information was found which linked the murder to an attack on one Mary O'Connor, a Romford schoolgirl, in the previous year. She had been attacked in a wood near Romford in June 1930, was stripped almost naked and left unconscious. Her attacker, perhaps one George McCarthy, had not been found. The difficulty was that witnesses had only caught a fleeting glimpse of a man whom the police wanted to question, and their descriptions of him were thus poor. Another witness came forward. She was a servant once employed in the Blackheath district but now working in the West End. She had told her priest about a man she thought might be the murderer. The priest persuaded her to reveal this information to the authorities, but it was discovered that her story was a mere fabrication to embarrass another man.

Senior police officers had located, in an unspecified place outside London, a pair of mudstained trousers, a cap and a pair of men's heavy boots. These would be tested in case they yielded any clues. It was possible that the kicks inflicted on Louisa's body were inflicted by a special type of heavy footwear. The press was led to understand that further enquiries were made in the country, but that further local developments were not being ruled out. Unfortunately, none of these leads seemed to go anywhere.

The police believed that the murder was 'actuated by a strong motive'. They ruled out the crime as being the work of a 'mental degenerate'. They believed that the murder took place away from Blackheath and then the corpse was driven to the Heath and bundled onto the ground. They also believed that Louisa, who was given considerable liberty by her employer, often went for walks on the Heath, and it may have been the case that she struck up a friendship with someone she met there, someone quite unknown to anyone else.

Press speculation, however, was that the killer must be a lunatic. It was supposed that the man was a 'border-line' case and that anyone who knew anyone with such tendencies should report him. They surmised that the killer might be in other ways perfectly normal, but suffered from blackouts in which he could not remember anything. It was also thought the attacks on the women earlier in the evening were by the same man and that, if Louisa had not been killed, then another woman would have been.

Psychological profiling of criminals is not a modern phenomenon. Spilsbury was interviewed by the press and gave his thoughts about the type of man the police sought. He would be a shy, outwardly respectable young man, who did not make close friends easily. He might have been betrayed by a girl in the past and now sought revenge (which sounds much like William Udall in the previous chapter). He would probably strike again.

Who did kill Louisa Steele? There have been three suggestions which have been made, two on the same theme and a third which is inconclusive.

In 1932, Superintendent Arthur Neil of Scotland Yard wrote the following comment in his memoirs about the murder:

> *The murderer is still at large. It is understood in well informed circles that an educated man of a well to do family was strongly suspected. But proof was lacking. It was known that this man had been an inmate in a mental institution and had several times been discharged on parole as recovered. And committed to the care of his own people. Immediately after the crime he was back again in his private mental home, and the authorities will see to it that he does not come out again.*

Yet as we shall note, Neil was not revealing the whole truth, of which he, as a senior officer, must have been aware.

Likewise, in a biography of Sir Bernard Spilsbury, written two decades later, the authors make the following similar observation; regrettably unsourced, so its provenance is unknown.

> *The man who killed her had been released from a mental home, presumably as cured, but his own family were so frightened of him that they would not have him in the house, and it was on their information that the police detained him on another charge before he could kill again. He was sent to Broadmoor.*

Again, there is some truth in this. Both these accounts are remarkably reticent over the killer's identity and the events leading up to the murder. It is generally assumed that this is an unsolved mystery, and the interested reader must either accept one of the above conclusions or formulate his own. Unfortunately, as is often the case with unsolved mysteries (Jack the Ripper being the obvious example), the killer was not motivated by any rational motive such as jealousy, fear or greed, and so their identity is not restricted to a small number of possible suspects, often within the victim's circle of family, friends and acquaintances. It could have been anyone, though was probably a man, motivated by some kind of sexual and sadistic lust. It had been Louisa's fatal misfortune to be in the wrong place at the wrong time.

The case was briefly reopened by one Tony Lord in a local newspaper in 1991. He revealed that one Arthur James Faraday Salvage, a twenty-three-year-old poultry farmer of Ashford, had killed an eleven-year-old girl, Ivy Godden, in the same neighbourhood as himself on 5 July 1931. After having been found guilty on 16 September, he was sentenced to death. He had once lived in Tresillian Road, Brockley, and this petty criminal had confessed to the murder of Louisa Steele while in Brixton prison, awaiting the gallows. Indeed, had the man not been found guilty of killing Ivy Godden, he would have been charged with the earlier murder.

Yet Lord did not think Salvage was guilty. He wrote 'People walk into police stations every day and confess to crimes they haven't committed. It brings these inadequates a brief spell of notoriety and attention.' Lord thought it unlikely that a petty criminal with a record of bag snatching would turn to murder and that he would travel to Blackheath from Ashford and back on a cold night. The police, he said, had little proof. Another crime writer stated 'inquiry showed that he could have had nothing to do with the crime, his confession being only another example of exhibitionism very common among persons of unstable mind'.

In any case, Lord referred to the case of a woman who was attacked on the Heath in 1937, but was rescued. He surmised that the assailant, who 'had an awful face', might have been the same man who killed Miss Steele, 'the man with the twisted lip'. Lord stated this could not be Salvage as he was already dead (having been executed, or so Lord surmised). He finally added, the hypothetical question 'Are you still out there, Louisa's killer – an old man in your eighties nursing your grisly secret?' However, as we shall see, Lord was mistaken.

All of the three hypotheses contain an element of truth, but none are complete.

The Heath remained a place of fear. Small children avoided playing near to where the corpse was found. A newspaper in 1937 referred to the case thus 'the evil work of some person who has never yet been brought to justice'. Despite the extra policing there,

Nevertheless, many women are very loth to venture on the heath at night. Its evil reputation still lingers; the memory of that unsolved murder of less than seven years ago is not easily effaced.

Women travelled across the Heath after dark in organized groups. Had the author of this book known of this crime when he crossed the Heath late one winter's night in 1995 he might have thought twice – but at least he was armed with a sword.

What is interesting to note is that Louisa's last journey was along well lit, well populated streets. She would have walked northwards along Lee Road, then through Blackheath Village and then to Tranquil Vale, to the chemists there. At no time would her route have led her across the Heath. True, it was a dark January night, but it seems strange that no one saw her and no one heard her cry out. For some reason she must have walked on to the Heath of her own free will. This begs the question why. Exercise? To meet someone? Both seem unlikely. Perhaps someone induced her to walk there – her killer, though she was not to know that. A writer on crime noted, in a book published in 1960, after noting the inconclusive nature of the inquest, wrote 'And that is the last that has ever been heard of the matter.'

This might indeed have been the last word on the subject, had it not been for the contents of two files created by the Metropolitan Police and the Home Office, but once completely closed until 2010. Fortunately, under Freedom of Information legislation, most of these files are now in the public domain and so the truth can now be told – not the whole truth, as pages from one of the files are still secret for another few years, but at last a solution can be arrived at. This information was not available to Lord nor to any other of the previous investigators.

It has already been noted that in July the police claimed to be following a new lead out in the country. This was true, but was never fully made public. A number of newspapers, *The Evening News, The Daily Mail, The Daily Sketch* and *The Kentish Mercury*, ran the story, in September 1931, that Salvage had confessed to the murder. Not all newspapers carried this story – *The Times* did not, perhaps because there was some doubt over its veracity.

According to statements made by the police, this was not the end of the story. One newspaper quoted an anonymous senior official at Scotland Yard as stating 'The mystery is not yet solved'. This individual claimed there were more avenues to be explored in order to find the killer. But there was a gap between what the police said in public and what they thought in private.

What had happened was that an anonymous letter was received by the investigating detectives, sent from Hampstead on 9 July. It read: 'Salvage, the Ashford murderer, formerly lived at Blackheath, and may very well be responsible for the unsolved murder of the girl on the Common.' As noted, Salvage had been arrested for the murder of Ivy Godden; this occurred on 7 July. The police were anxious to follow up any possible lead after Miss Steele's killer. On further investigation in Ashford, Detective Inspector Clark uncovered more facts. Salvage had been released from Borstal on 5 December 1930. What was new was that he had been strongly suspected of assaulting two women near Ashford earlier in that year: Miss Jordan and Mrs Anne Allright. In one instance, he had torn off most of one of his victim's clothing. Unfortunately, he was never charged with either offence. Salvage had been at Ruckinge on 23 December 1930, but although his devoted widowed mother vouched for him on the night of the Blackheath murder, Mrs Forster, a neighbour, 'missed Salvage altogether for several days'. Apparently he came around to their house each day to shave her ill husband, but had failed to turn up in late January.

It was also discovered that Salvage knew the Blackheath district reasonably well. First, he knew Mr Milner, a solicitor, who lived at Vanburgh Hill in Blackheath and also had a house in Ruckinge. Secondly, Salvage had not only lived in the neighbourhood once, but had also worked in Greenwich for the Telegraph Maintenance and Construction Company and had played football for Westcombe Park Rugby Football Club. Salvage had had a good education, was a clever and industrious draughtsman, a cricketer and a churchgoer.

Superintendent Cooper visited Salvage in Brixton prison on 13 July, but Salvage told him that his solicitor had told him to say nothing. He later said that, although he knew Blackheath, he had not been there since about 1925. However, an identity parade was set up. Neither of the two women attacked near Blackheath on the night of the murder picked him out. Yet Miss Chinnicke did, saying 'he was very like the man she had seen attack one of the women'. The police also thought he matched the description of the wanted man.

It was not until 7 August that the police heard from Salvage. The latter wrote to the Assistant Commissioner of Scotland Yard thus: 'I understand that it has nothing to do with the charge for which I am in here now, it is the Blackheath crime. I did it.' The detectives returned to interview him and asked him for the particulars of the crime. Salvage told them: 'No, I don't want to tell you any of the details, I know I did it and you must take it at that.' However, he did sign a statement. He said that on 22 January he travelled from Ashford to New Cross by train. He walked to the Heath and wandered over it, passing All Saints' Church. Salvage then said,

> I crossed the road and got onto the grass and walked along towards where this round about thing for buses is. I saw the girl coming towards me. She was walking on the footpath. When she passed me I turned around and caught her by the throat with my hands the same as I did this time at Ashford. I don't remember anything more until I saw her lying in the grass.

Salvage recalled covering her up with her coat and then running away, towards Messrs Keatings Ltd, a wireless shop on Westcoombe Hill. He did not recall reaching home, but assumed he must have caught a train to do so. It could not have been on the night of the murder, because the last train had already gone by 9 pm. Salvage claimed he suffered from fits of depression, or as he said, he 'came over queer', and could not recall attacking the other two women either.

Was there any corroborating evidence? His clothes and footwear were tested by Dr Lynch, but no traces of blood could be found. Nor did the soles of his shoes yield anything, though they were studded with small nails – ideal for kicking a victim. It was, after all, six months after the murder.

There was, however, an additional, and most macabre, clue. Salvage had talked to his fellow prisoners about biting off the nipples of Ivy Godden. But she had not been mutilated. However, as will be recalled, Miss Steele's breasts had been mutilated – no further detail was given. Spilsbury's confidential report did most crucially mention that Miss Steele's nipples had been bitten off. Only her murderer could have known that. This gruesome act has been known to have been carried out by later serial killers. Yet a pencilled comment on the file's margin casts a little doubt on this, 'I am afraid it did become common knowledge.'

Superintendent Cooper wrote: 'I feel convinced that Salvage was telling the truth when he confessed to having committed the Blackheath murder.' His evidence was as follows. Salvage was away from home on the night of the killing; he had a history of attacking women and fitted the description given of the assailant; indeed Miss Chinnicke recognized him. His fellow convicts recounted the story about his macabre mutilations and he knew about injuries that only the killer could have known. Finally, the reason for the confession was so that no one else was convicted for the murder he was responsible for. He had nothing to gain by the confession. Cooper's colleague agreed with the assessment, writing:

> In view of all the known facts concerning this man, it would appear that we must accept his confession as a genuine one, and that he murdered Miss Steele in the same manner as he murdered Ivy Godden, as he described it 'under an uncontrollable impulse'. I know Superintendent Cooper is convinced he is responsible for our crime, especially with the Ashford one.

It is also worth noting that Spilsbury's profile of the killer was remarkably accurate.

Salvage was never tried for the Blackheath murder. There was no need. In September, he was found guilty of the Ashford murder and sentenced to death, but (contrary to the aforesaid Lord) was reprieved on 2 October. He was deemed to be insane and was committed to Broadmoor on the following day. He died there in 1966. Unfortunately, access to his file held there has been denied, so it is only possible to surmise about Salvage's mental condition. He may have been showered with excessive maternal affection (his father died when he was young) and might have been a loner and unconfident with women, which are traits of serial killers, as is killing in districts well known to them. His previous history of petty crime is also a characteristic of men of this type. He may also have killed for the pleasure it gave him. That he was mentally disturbed had been noted as long ago as 1927 and he had been recognized as such by medical staff at a mental institute in Hull. It was noted that he struggled violently and later could not recall what happened. This behaviour is exactly the same as described above – violence towards Louisa and then forgetting what happened next (he made similar statements about the two women in Kent). Although staff recommended he be sent to an asylum, he was not because he made a speedy recovery. Indeed, immediately prior to his trial for killing Ivy Godden, Dr Grierson (lacking the above information) noted that Salvage was not insane. Salvage clearly had a 'Jekyll and Hyde' persona.

Oddly enough, the file on the Blackheath murder remained open until the following decade. A number of people were reported as being allegedly involved in the murder – usually by others who held grudges against them or allegations were made by people who were 'unbalanced'. These continued until 1946 and were all followed up; wasting police resources but maintaining the illusion that the case was unsolved.

The question of Salvage's confession was raised by Sir Assheton Pownall, MP for Lewisham East (the constituency where the murder occurred), with Sir Simon Anderson, Under Secretary for the Home Office, in September 1931. Anderson stated:

> There is no doubt that he [Salvage] committed these and other crimes. As however he has been certified insane, I doubt whether he can properly or easily make a statement; many people would think it unfair and unjust to make it on the strength of a lunatic's confession; his mother would undoubtedly resent it. Someone else might at some other time pretend to make a similar statement on strength of mere meanderings; the people of Blackheath can draw their own conclusions from publications concerning the confessions. The public, are, I think, fairly satisfied with the statements in the press as to Salvage having confessed to the murders.

It seems reasonably certain that Salvage was indeed the murderer of Miss Steele, though the full story was withheld from the public by the police. Why was this? It surely would have been a feather in the cap of Cooper and his colleagues to have caught the killer of a girl whose death had received national press coverage. It is possible that if they had been seen to have done so, the police would have been criticized. After all, the Ashford Police knew that Salvage had attacked two women in 1930. Had they told this to their colleagues investigating the Blackheath murder, Salvage would have been brought in and therefore Ivy Godden's life would have been saved. The reason why information was not passed on was because Superintendent Pattenden of the Ashford force had retired and his successor, Robertson, who took over in November 1930, was unaware of Salvage's past record. This would have looked bad if it had been made public. Therefore, it was preferable that the public think the murder was unsolved, whereas in fact it had and the killer was safely locked away in Broadmoor, bringing his murderous career to a halt.

CHAPTER **23**

Who Killed Robert Venner?
1934

We went up there but the old man got a bit naughty and had to be cracked ...

On the early evening of Friday 6 July 1934, Robert James Venner, the middle-aged manager of Henry Cohen's tailor's shop on New Cross Road, was alone in the shop. That was unfortunate for him, for he was attacked by a man who was posing as a customer. His assailant then apparently drove away from the scene of the crime in a car towards the Old Kent Road, in the direction of the Bricklayers' Arms. Venner staggered about the shop, coatless and covered in blood. He was in a dazed condition and could not speak. John Bell, a maker of perambulators and invalid coaches, was passing by at about 6.20 pm and looked through the shop window. Shocked at the sight, he opened the door and said, 'Hullo. What is the matter?'

Venner made no reply. He walked away from Bell and wiped his face several times, before then walking towards Bell. It was then that Bell called the police. They tried to get Venner to sit down, but he kept walking around the shop. Venner had been terribly battered, with blood running from his head. He had probably been hit six times with an iron bar. He was taken to the Miller Hospital in Greenwich, though he struggled wildly, leading some to doubt his sanity. Five days later, he died in hospital without regaining consciousness and so was unable to give a description of his attackers to the detectives who waited at his bedside for such information. His employer, for whom Venner had worked since 1908, said Venner was 'a man of the highest possible character'.

Superintendent Hulbey of Scotland Yard led the investigation. There were a number of leads to follow up. There were descriptions of the men thought to be those responsible. They were 'believed to be well known in certain districts of London'. The killer was said to be about forty years old, five feet five inches in height, clean shaven, with a broken nose, broad build and tattooed arms. He was last seen wearing a grey suit and was 'known to be a frequenter of race meetings'. However, another description of his clothing was that he was wearing a blue jacket and waistcoat, flannel trousers and was hatless. He was said to be slimly built, not well built. There was blood on his hands and on his trousers. Of the other men, the car driver, who had kept the engine running during the attack, had a bluish overcoat, white muffler and brown trilby hat, pulled down at the front. A third man wore a light mackintosh and cap. Lodging houses and cafes in Soho and elsewhere in London were combed by officers of the Flying Squad, but to no apparent avail.

Then there were a number of physical clues. First, there was the tailor's book in the shop. This recorded all the measurements of customers of the shop's goods, including the last one ever taken by Venner. It gave the name of a Mr J.C. Robinson at Alfred Road, Brockley. Alas, upon investigation, the address was false and there was no Mr Robinson nor ever had been. A total of 350 people were questioned, including local thieves, past employees, customers, shop-keepers and drivers of trams and buses. One Mrs Gardner described three men leaving the shop and said that one was 'deathly white – like a corpse'. One Oliver Cross said he saw a man with something concealed under his coat leave the premises.

Secondly, a bloodstained jacket had been bought on a market stall in Douglas Street, Deptford, on the morning after the assault. This

New Cross Road, c.1908. London Borough of Lewisham

was given to the police by its new owner and examined by experts at Scotland Yard. Lodging houses, coffee stalls and laundries in south-east London were visited by detectives, hoping to follow up this lead.

Another possible clue was that a curious gold brooch, the size of a shilling, set with a diamond, used to adorn the lapel of Venner's coat, and two gold rings of the snake design, with rubies and diamonds for eyes, which he used to wear, were missing. Jewellers, pawnbrokers and gold refiners were questioned – again, with little result. However, it was thought that this jewellery had already been sold by Venner, who was in need of money.

The getaway car had been described. It was a new light-blue saloon model with a false aluminium number plate, which began with the letters AN (the numbers were not noticed). The car had large glazed headlights and plated bumpers, both back and front. It was thought that the car had been disposed of after the attack and so garage proprietors in south London were questioned by detectives. An appeal was put out by the BBC.

Unfortunately, cumulative progress was limited, as a local newspaper commented:

> *The New Cross Gate murder mystery is assuming a problem of growing magnitude. There have been no dearth of clues, but all the ingenuity of Scotland Yard and the local police as yet has been of no avail. The murderer is still at large, and, according to the information available, there seems to be no hopeful signs of an early arrest.*

The inquest was delayed until 24 August – an unusually long time after the murder. Herbert Burrows, who worked at the branch of Barclay's bank nearby, reported last seeing Venner in the doorway of the shop at 6.00 pm. He recalled Venner saying to him, 'You lucky beggar, to be finished at this time of day'. Burrows replied, 'You wait until I come back'.

He did not notice anyone hanging about outside the shop, but in any case, was unlikely to do, as it was next to a tram stop, it was a busy thoroughfare. He added that Venner was often alone in the shop, but he never mentioned being threatened by any shady customers. Mrs Emma Venner, the dead man's widow, agreed that her late husband had never mentioned anything which might throw a light on the murder.

No weapon was ever found. Dr Arthur Davies, a Harley Street pathologist, had examined the corpse and found there to be seven separate blows to the head. The brain had also been lacerated and there was an abrasion on the jaw, possibly caused by a fist. Venner had been struck down suddenly and had been unable to defend himself.

Dr Davies thought that the wounds were inflicted when Venner was in a stooping position, perhaps when measuring a trouser leg.

Theft was almost certainly the motive. There was no till in the shop, but there might have been only about £5 on the premises, trade being slack, and some small change remained on Venner's person. The coroner suggested that the killing might not be murder and that there might have been extenuating circumstances which were currently unknown, and therefore the man involved should come forward and make a clean breast of matters. He also asked the jury if they wished to postpone their verdict for a week or two, in case any more information became available. They did not require this. They decided that Venner died of injuries caused by a blunt instrument, inflicted by person or persons unknown.

Yet, a few months later, it appeared that the end might be in sight. Percy John McGee, a thirty-six-year-old plumber of Glenton Road, Lee, went to Lee Police Station on 30 September and gave himself up as the murderer. A statement was taken and he was detained. He claimed that Gerald, his brother, and a man named Jack Martin had killed Venner. McGee claimed to have visited the shop on the pretence of being measured for a suit. Whilst Venner saw to this, Gerald and Martin rushed in and 'bashed the tailor'. The police thought the statement was doubtful and made enquiries. A few days later, McGee admitted it was a hoax:

> *All I have told you is a pack of lies. I know nothing about the murder beyond what I read in the papers. I took no part in it nor, so far as I know, did my brother Gerald or Jack Martin. I mentioned their names as I owe them a grudge and I thought they might as well have a bit of trouble.*

The police were not happy. McGee was charged 'with doing an act which tended to produce a public mischief' by wasting police time and money and imperilling the liberty of two innocent men.

What was the truth of this shocking and brutal crime? This was a theft which went wrong. The crime seems to have been planned, as the getaway car was ready for a quick escape. The men had doubtless been watching the shop for some time and one had come especially armed. They had chosen a time when Venner was alone and vulnerable. These were professional thieves from London and appear to have escaped quite easily. No one was ever charged with the murder.

Recently available police files throw a new light on the case and offer a solution. They have never before been made public and will now be surveyed.

The case remained open until at least 1941. In the years following 1934, a number of suggestions were sent to the police, which is usual after any unsolved crime. One correspondent told the police about a similar crime in Brighton and an anonymous postcard suggested 'It will pay you to look after a man named Fred'. Charles Pearson, a prisoner in Pentonville Gaol told how a fellow inmate, one Bailey, with whom he discussed the New Cross murder, told him 'It's funny, I thought I would have been called on the mat for it.' Bailey, however, was mentally deficient; as was one Thomas Marchant who told the police in 1938 that he had relevant information. The last accusation came in 1941 when Mrs Charlton and William Jordan pointed the finger at Rodney Pharoah, aged nineteen in 1934, and who had worked at Deptford Cattle Market. Apparently he had absented himself from work at the time of the killing and allegedly resembled the killer. The police, after investigation, concluded this was merely 'idle talk over the tea table'.

Yet, as in the case of the Louisa Steele murder in 1931, while the police in public claimed the investigation was still being continued, the real culprit's identity was, in all probability, known to them. It was stated, in 1935 that the case was 'still actively pursued but so far no tangible information has come to hand'.

There was much that the police did not make public. First, one of the statements they took was from a Joseph Neale, a racing tipster then living in a common lodging house in Barlow Street, Walworth. He told them that he had seen three men leave the shop, noted blood seeping under the shop's door and later saw Venner being removed into an ambulance at 7.00 pm. He also told that he went to the newspapers first about his story in order to try and gain some money, before reporting it to the police.

Police suspicion pointed towards him, as the following extract from the official confidential report of 13 August 1934 (i.e. before the inquest was held) notes:

> *shortly afterwards, it was common knowledge amongst the underworld of this district that Neale was thought to be closely associated with this crime. I later saw a number of well known thieves and caused careful enquiries to be made at cafes and lodging houses in this district and the whole of the information thus obtained strongly pointed to Neale as a suspect.*

Evidence against Neale came from a number of sources. One was his estranged wife, Louisa, who told police that on 9 July, that her husband told her:

> *I've got mixed up in a bit of trouble at New Cross. I saw some blood in the shop and I saw a tall man hopping about and then they ran out. A man got knocked down at New Cross, but they only got £6.*

Louisa replied: 'I expect you were the outside man.' Later that day, a friend of Neale's visited Louisa and warned her about approaching the police, 'If you go saying that Joe is the outside man, Joe says he will kick you up the c***'. Neale was a violent man, having assaulted his wife two months previously, so this was no idle threat.

Another source of evidence against Neale was Frederick Evans, a former criminal (having nine previous convictions) and informant. He said he was not surprised that Neale was involved and added that 'Charlie the Navvy' was involved, and that 'Flash Joe' from the West End was the third of the trio.

Neale was pulled in for questioning. Initially he told the police: 'You're mad ... I can tell you everything I did on that day, and account for my movements right up to a minute. It will be a long story.' He claimed he had spent the day of the crime selling racing tips in pubs and cafes. In the early evening he had been in the vicinity of the Old Kent Road, and had witnessed aspects of the crime, as previously noted. He had then spent the remainder of the day in a café. He had worn a brown jacket, a blue raincoat, grey trousers and a grey cap.

Charles Nougher, an unemployed labourer aged thirty-three, and identified by Evans, was also questioned. He lived in the same lodging house as Neale. As with Neale, he denied all knowledge of the crime. As a start, he claimed 'Neale and I have not been friendly for a long time and I know nothing about his movements.' He said he had stayed in until 11.00 am, when he had visited the Labour Exchange, then returned and went out to a number of pubs in the evening. Apparently, the first he knew of the affair was on the following day when he had heard others mentioning Neale's name in connection with it.

The final suspect, Joseph Gibbons, 'Flash Joe', a costermonger at Paddington, was also questioned. He simply claimed 'I know nothing about it'. All three men were lined up in identity parades, but none of the witnesses picked them out. Furthermore, on 23 July, when Neale's clothes were tested for bloodstains, none could be found.

It is also unclear whether the criminals escaped using a car, as the press had maintained, as there is no mention of one in the police file on the crime. It seems unlikely that the three men would have had access to one. Witnesses may have been mistaken. They probably escaped on foot.

Yet the circumstantial evidence against Neale and Nougher was strong. Further questioning of Evans revealed much that incriminated them. He recalled that on the day prior to the crime, Neale said to Nougher, 'We are going up to New Cross tomorrow night to get measured for a suit'. Evans recalled all three of them in a café on the morning of the crime. A week after the crime, they asked Evans to supply them with an alibi. Nougher told him, 'You know Joe and I told you last week that we were going up to New Cross to get measured for a suit. We went up there and the old man got a bit naughty and had to be cracked.' Although Evans refused, he also refused to give an official statement to the police for fear of reprisals.

It was not only Evans's word against Neale. One Perry Elliott, a fellow inmate with Neale, told how Neale confided in him thus, 'They roped me in for the New Cross Murder but I put up an alibi as to where I was.' Neale also said that they only took £6 and some cloth. Both Neale and Nougher were known criminals. Neale had had ten previous convictions, including two for assault. He was also known to beat his wife. Nougher only had two previous convictions, one being for shoplifting.

The police were fairly certain that Neale was guilty, though less so concerning Nougher. Their reasons were as follows. Neale's account of blood running under the door of the shop was impossible because the doorway was lower than the pavement. Mr Lyons, who Neale relied on for his alibi, denied that he had been buying racing tips from him. The measurements for the suit in the order book in the shop fitted those of Neale. Elliott's evidence also pointed towards him. They were on weaker ground concerning Nougher, but found he lacked the alibi he claimed he had. In fact, Nougher had asked a fellow lodger, John Murray, for an alibi after the crime, asking him 'I've got pulled in for the New Cross job. You know where I was, don't you, in the evening.' Unfortunately Murray said that he had not seen Nougher in the Marquis of Granby pub until after 7.00 pm; thus after the time of the crime. Finally, it was shown that they had lied over not being friends, as fellow lodgers spoke of their having conversations with one another.

The police report concluded:

> *I would suggest that the evidence amassed against the men, Neale and Nougher, points very clearly to the fact that they are beyond all reasonable doubt, the persons who committed the crime, but there may not be thought to be sufficient evidence for police to institute proceedings at this stage.*

This was the unfortunate reality. It was probably the reason why the inquest was delayed for so long – the police hoped to have information to put before the jury. Alas, they had not. Neither man had been picked out by the witnesses at the identity parades. Bloodstains had not been found on Neale's clothing. Evans refused to make an official statement against them. Although enquiries continued, nothing more concrete was discovered and so, although the police were fairly certain as to who killed Venner, the case was never cleared up and no one was ever officially charged. The public were, of course, in ignorance of the true state of affairs, but the reason why two vicious criminals walked free was not because they were innocent but because there was insufficient evidence to bring the case to court.

As Superintendent Neil wrote in 1932, 'Would it surprise the public to know that in a good many cases, they [the police] do trace the murderer – and then cannot prove his guilt?'

CHAPTER 24

The Queer Pastimes of William Brown
1938

... a man of sadistic tendencies, invariably in the company of young lads ...

I t is probable that Mr and Mrs Aldham, of Edward Street in New Cross, did not know very much about William England Brown, one of their lodgers. After all, he paid the rent on time (6*s* 6*d* per week) and kept himself largely to himself in the first-floor room he had rented from them since 1937. Brown was a middle-aged man when they first knew him, and was a civil engineer by profession, which all seemed above board. Physically he was unimpressive; 'a thin sallow faced man with a bald head'.

Unfortunately, that was not all. Brown had been born in Wales in 1890 and never married. He had a history of petty crime. In 1923 he had been sentenced to a month's hard labour for stealing ten shillings from a lodging house in Maesteg. More seriously, in 1935, he had used a knife to wound two youths and received twelve months' hard labour.

Brown's employment history was also unfortunate. Until 1927 he had worked at the Celtic Colliery at Maesteg, as an engineer, then at another Welsh colliery, before coming to London in 1928. Here he worked for Messrs A Jackman & Sons at the docks. He had suffered a head injury in 1930 when he had been hurt cycling home. Since then he had been unemployed and depended on payments given to the long-term unemployed. In 1938, he was being treated at Guy's Hospital for insomnia, brought on by depression and headache due to the earlier injury. He also suffered from stomach problems and nervous disorders.

After Brown had been at Edward Street for about three months, the police later stated:

Mrs Aldham states he commenced bringing young boys home and taking them into his room. The boys were usually brought home in the

evening and did not stay in the room very long. Mrs Aldham is certain
that on no occasion had any of the boys stayed all night.

It should be recalled that committing homosexual acts was illegal at this time. Yet few landladies were or are willing to turn away reliable paying tenants except for very good reasons.

It was in October 1937 that Brown found a longer term companion. This was one Alfred David Brown (no relation), a seventeen year old, who lived with his parents in Cranfield Road, Brockley, and worked for a tobacconist in New Cross. He had once been in trouble with the law for taking part in the theft of a car. Initially the two went to the cinema together, but from December the lad would visit about two or three times in the week. Eventually he let himself in, presumably with a key the elder Brown had copied for him. Now he would come up most nights, staying from about 6.30 to 9.00 pm. Mostly the two were very quiet.

Brown's landlady was concerned, but her lodger told him that 'there was no harm in it'. But matters became worse. On 17 April, she heard a series of bumpings in the room and tried to enter, but found she was unable to do so. The door was held shut, as it turned out by William Brown. Eventually she entered and saw the two Browns.

She asked them what they had been doing hitherto, 'What's the game?' She did not receive an answer from her lodger, but the lad

Cranfield Road, c.1900. London Borough of Lewisham

spoke up, 'He won't let me go.' Probably not entirely satisfied, she left the room and, half an hour later, the two Browns left together.

Two days later, they were together again in the room from about 6.00 pm. As before, there was a lot of noise emanating from the room. Mrs Aldham shouted up at them, 'If you can't make a little less noise, the young fellow will have to go and he won't have to come back here any more.' There was then rather less noise and Mrs Aldham settled downstairs again.

It was, however, only a lull. This time Mrs Aldham went upstairs and opened the door to see a shocking sight. The lad was lying on the floor, between the table and the fireplace. There was a pool of blood by his head. Mrs Aldham addressed Brown:

Whatever have you done?
Bleeding well done for him.
What?
I've cut his head off.

An obvious exaggeration, but in the circumstances, not surprising.

Mrs Aldham left the room and asked her other lodger, Miss Newman, to fetch the police. When she returned to the room, she asked,

What have you really done?
You don't know what he has done to me.

She left the room again, followed by Brown who announced, 'I am going to give myself up'. The landlady told him, 'You are not going outside this door'.

By now the police had begun to arrive, in the shape of Detective Sergeants Allcock and Meldrum. They examined the lad's wounds, which were on his neck and wrist. Meanwhile, Brown had collapsed on the bed. The injured youth told them, 'He's stabbed me with a knife and he has taken poison. He's got a kink [a mental oddity].' Brown interjected with, 'I don't know why I did it. I must be mad. God forgive me for what I have done.' He added that he loved Alfred and continued to say 'why did I do it?' often. Inspector Warlow and Dr Danin arrived. The latter made several attempts to revive the younger man, but without success and he had to be taken to Miller Hospital. Afterwards, the police searched the room for anything incriminating.

William Brown was not found to have taken poison, but Alfred had been badly hurt, having lost two pints of blood from two deep wounds on the right side of his neck, as well as a less deep wound on his wrist. In hospital, he told Sergeant Meldrum:

Edward Street, 2006. The author

We had a bit of a quarrel and he stabbed me. He suffers a lot and didn't want to leave me to go to hospital. He always carries a knife. I was not there for anything wrong, don't think that.

Alfred's father, Frederick Brown, a forty-five-year-old tram driver, had no idea about his son's friendship with the older man. He had never met William Brown, and had assumed that his son was seeing a friend of the same age or was spending his time at cinemas with a girlfriend. In Alfred's pocket was found a letter dated 8 April from William Brown, though its contents may not be accurate. Part of it read:

am sorry that our friendship has to end, but as I don't want to get you into any unpleasant trouble this is why I write this statement . . . I have on no occasion given you money. You have visited me here as my friend.

However, on 20 April Alfred died at Greenwich Hospital of broncho-pneumonia brought on by the stabbing.

Brown was accused on 27 April at Greenwich Magistrates' Court and was remanded for trial. He was held at Brixton Prison. Through-out the questioning, he pleaded that he had not meant to kill Brown. On 20 April, he said, 'I did not mean to do him any harm.' When asked about murder, he replied, 'I plead not guilty to that. I did it in self defence. He tried to choke me on the bed.'

Divisional Detective Inspector Arthur Dawson took a less chari-table view of Brown's character, stating: 'He is a man of sadistic tendencies, invariably in the company of young lads with whom he seems to delight in conversing of sexual matters.'

It seems that relations between the two were certainly difficult. Brown was clearly emotionally attached to the younger man, once saying 'Why did I do it? I love him', but also denied there was any-thing 'improper' in his conduct, or as he explicitly stated at one point, there was nothing pertaining to a 'sexual relation'. Yet despite his statement in the letter that money had not passed between them, he later claimed that it had. Apparently Alfred would ask for money and, if refused, threatened to expose Brown's criminal past. Brown sold his wireless and pawned clothes in order to meet these demands. On the day of the assault, Brown had no more money to give and told Alfred that he had written to the lad's father asking him to keep Alfred away from him or both Browns would get into trouble. Feeling deprived of money and threatened, Alfred became angry and threatened to kill Brown, who was physically weaker than he.

Dr Hugh Grierson examined Brown to check he was sane and therefore able to stand trial. Although one of Brown's brothers was in a mental hospital, there was no history of mental illness in the family. Grierson thought though Brown was 'a man of weak character, emotional and neurotic, he has not shown signs of suffering from such disease of the mind as would prevent him knowing what he was doing'.

On 17 May, Brown was tried at the Old Bailey for murder. He pleaded not guilty: that he acted merely in self-defence and that in the struggle Alfred was accidentally wounded. The court found him guilty, but recommended he be granted mercy because of his poor physical health. The death sentence was then passed, at which Brown shrieked and groaned and had to be carried from the courtroom. He was to be executed at Wandsworth Prison on 8 June. However, one week before this was to have happened, he was granted a reprieve and was sentenced to penal servitude for life (i.e. imprisonment with hard labour).

We will never know what really happened in Brown's room on the fatal night. It may have been self-defence, as Brown said. Alfred may have wanted to kill him because his source of money had dried up and he was being threatened. On the other hand, the older man did have a record of assaulting young men and was being blackmailed. Passions of a kind or kinds were certainly high. It was right that Brown was given the benefit of the doubt, but of course he may have stabbed Alfred maliciously and with intent – he had the motive – but despite being bled dry he also had tender feelings towards him.

Conclusion

his has not been an exhaustive account of all serious crimes in Lewisham and Deptford's history before 1939. An elderly couple were killed in their house by burglars in Deptford in 1776, a Sydenham man shot dead another later in the century and in 1920 a former Canadian soldier shot a woman dead in a house on whose site now stands Millwall Football Ground. A spurned lover killed his former mistress, then slit his own throat in Forest Hill in 1913. At least two local women killed their own children in the nineteenth century. This is quite apart from less serious crimes – vagrancy, drunkenness, begging, theft and assault.

Here follows a little analysis of the sample of murders discussed in this book. Of the killers, they were overwhelmingly male, as should be expected: sixteen in all, only one was female. Thirteen victims were killed by knives and another six were bludgeoned. Five were poisoned, and in one case a gun was used; in another a stone was used and in another the victim was strangled. Motives for murder were equally varied – insanity resulted in nine deaths, and the financial factor led to an equal number. Hostility to authority led to the killings of three men; revenge resulted in Patrick Desmond's death and the motive for two killings are unknown.

Detection varied. Often there was none needed – in several cases the killers gave themselves up to the police, as in the cases chronicled here in 1897, 1919 and 1926. Other men were caught due to informers or their colleagues who turned King's Evidence, as in 1776 and 1822. Few were solved by detection, except in the case of the Deptford poisoners in 1889 and the Strattons in 1905. In four, though the police were able to identify the killer/s, there was insufficient evidence to convict – as in 1845, 1868, 1931 and 1934.

Of the killers, four were hanged and six sent to Broadmoor. Two were gaoled, one went untried, one was acquitted, one was transported, one escaped and one died before being tried. None committed suicide, interestingly enough. Of their victims, ten were men, nine were women and five were children. We do not know who two of Mrs Winters's victims were.

The past was not a golden age. As well as the actual crimes which have been related here, it will also have been noted that many involved in these dramas lived in poverty – the Cavillas, for instance, and also the Evendens. Of course, it can also be argued that violent crime is just as, if not greater, now than ever it was; nor is the end of poverty in

Contemporary murder in Lewisham, 2006. The author

sight. Certainly the statistics show that this is the case. In the 1920s there were only three murders in the locality and the same in the 1930s. Compare this to fourteen murders in the two-year period from March 2004 to March 2006. Since the population has fallen between these periods (286,768 in 1921 to 248,922 in 2001), the contrast is even more stark. The causes for this increase are for the reader to decide, but changes in society and the criminal justice system are probably to blame.

The impression is that Deptford was, at times, a very violent place; groups of men taking part in the killing of others, or in conspiracy of various kinds. It was a lawless place which was bloodily antagonistic towards the representatives of any form of law and order. Superintendent Thomas Divall later recalled 'no doubt Deptford was the rowdiest district in London'. As a new recruit there in the 1880s he was asked by his inspector if he could fight. When he replied in the affirmative, his superior said, 'That will just do for us'. Until the twentieth century, Lewisham was generally more peaceful, but became a little less so as its population rose and its social composition changed.

Index